Praise for *Cats on the Counter*

"I can't exaggerate in explaining what cats have meant to my life, from Flippy, my very first pet, who taught me that all living creatures have individual talent and souls, to Buttons, who endured a terrible accident and who graciously taught me patience, endurance, and courage while healing, to Connecticat, who at present travels with me everywhere and is my best friend. *Cats on the Counter* not only provides cat lovers with important information, but it reaffirms my belief that people are only experiencing themselves to the fullest when they care deeply about other life-forms." —Gary Burghoff, host of public television's *Pets: Part of the Family*, and "Radar" from the CBS television series *M*A*S*H*

"*Cats on the Counter* is an exceptionally clear, well-written, and helpful book that advocates the exemplary whole-family approach to resolving pet behavior problems. On a personal level, Larry Lachman and Frank Mickadeit's book will be of infinite value to me as I assist my canine clients who've been having trouble blending with their feline family members. What's more, this book makes even a total dog person like myself appreciate the cat psyche!"

—Allie Babcock (the fictional Ms. Babcock is a dog behaviorist and the main character in a mystery series created by author Leslie O'Kane, which includes the books *Play Dead* and *Ruff Way to Go*)

"They have done it again! Dr. Larry Lachman and Frank Mickadeit have met and exceeded the quality of their work in *Dogs on the Couch*. *Cats on the Counter* helps cat owners learn as much about themselves as they do about their feline companions. Inspired by the magic touch of a good storyteller, Dr. Larry Lachman and Frank Mickadeit inform, empower, and entertain all at the same time. This is a book that gives scientific psychology away. Bravo!" —Aghop Der-karabetian, Ph.D., professor of psychology, University of LaVerne, Southern California

"The behavioral complexities of the 'finicky feline' can create either the most special human-animal bond between species or a situation that could be described as antagonistic. Dr. Larry Lachman and Frank Mickadeit have again produced excellent reading not only for the novice but also for the lifelong cat lover. Whether you have a problem or just want a better understanding of your relationship with your cat, this book is a must-read for every cat lover." —Dr. Tom Schmar, host and producer of *Pet Connection with Dr. Tom Schmar*, Topeka, Kansas

ALSO BY DR. LARRY LACHMAN AND FRANK MICKADEIT

Dogs on the Couch: Behavior Therapy
for Training and Caring for Your Dog

CATS ON THE COUNTER

Therapy and Training for Your Cat

DR. LARRY LACHMAN AND FRANK MICKADEIT

St. Martin's Griffin ❧ New York

Note: All cat names and owner-identifying characteristics have been changed to protect the privacy of the families.

All photos by Robert Lachman except where noted

Book design by Casey Hampton

www.stmartins.com

Library of Congress Cataloging-in-Publication Data

Lachman, Larry.
    Cats on the counter : therapy and training for your cat / Larry Lachman
& Frank Mickadeit.
        p. cm.
    Includes bibliographical references (p.187–92).
    ISBN 0-312-26566-2 (hc)
    ISBN 0-312-28893-X (pbk)
    1. Cats—Behavior therapy. 2. Cats—Training. 3. Cats—Psychology.
4. Cat owners—Psychology. 5. Family psychotherapy. I. Mickadeit, Frank.
II. Title.
SF446.5 .L33 2000
636.8'0887—dc21   00-031741

First St. Martin's Griffin Edition: January 2002

10 9 8 7 6 5 4 3 2 1

To the cats I grew up knowing or who have been part of my household: Bibsy, a Russian blue; Blackie, a domestic longhair; Coal, a domestic shorthair; Angel, a tabby-and-white; and Bogie, a Turkish angora–exotic shorthair mix. Also to my many cat friends, past and present, especially Mori, Yuki, Beethoven, Gershwin, Kringle, Frasier, Oscar, Topaz, and Sheba. This book is for you, your people, and dedicated cat "guardians" everywhere! —Larry Lachman

To my late grandmother, Esther Parks, whose love for her cats, Cobina, Rastus, Muffy, and Tom, was second only to her love for her grandchildren. —Frank Mickadeit

CONTENTS

ACKNOWLEDGMENTS

In the human-behavior arena, I'd like to acknowledge Dr. Alfred Adler, Dr. Carl G. Jung, Dr. Salvador Minuchin, Dr. Aaron Beck, and Dr. B. F. Skinner.

In the cat-behavior arena, I'd like to acknowledge the influences of Dr. Michael W. Fox, Dr. Myrna Milani, Dr. John C. Wright, Carole C. Wilbourn, Ray Berwick, and Desmond Morris.

To those friends and/or cat owners who believed in this project from its inception without wavering and provided support and advice: Kimberly and Brian Akamine, Jim and Pam Carter, Dr. Kathleen Farinacci, Dr. Steve Feig, Stephen Biggs and Valerie Garcia, Deb and Drew Varos, Steve and Joanna Haddon, Patti and Chuck Leviton, Lori Osborne, Dr. Joel Pasco, Dr. Nancy Hauer, Dr. Eric Van Nice, Dr. Joe Cortese, Dr. Ronald Kelpe, Dr. David Gordon, Dr. Michelle McCann, Gary and Karen Zager, Sue Mulcahy, Dolores Heikes, Don Richardson, Paul Hayes, Maria Tello, Karen Commings, Jon Baker, Nancy Schlesinger, and Shirley Thayer.

Finally, I must recognize our editor at St. Martin's, Dorsey Mills; our agent, Barbara Braun; the photographer, Robert Lachman; Frank's wife, journalist Kathryn Bold, who proofread this manuscript as well as the many incarnations of the manuscript for *Dogs on the Couch*; and my parents, Leon and Joan, for believing in *Cats on the Counter* and for helping to make it happen. Thank you.

—*Larry Lachman*

FOREWORD

by Eric Van Nice, D.V.M.,
Olympiad Animal Hospital,
Mission Viejo, California

Pet behavior problems are some of the most frustrating and challenging facing veterinarians today. Here are some recent examples from my own practice:

In one case, we performed four root-canal procedures to save a cat's "fang" teeth. They had been cut down to the nubs because a previous owner had not been able to find any other alternative to make the cat stop biting her, and now the teeth were painfully infected.

In a second case, a couple brought in their beautiful Persian cat because it had been soiling the carpet. Examination of the cat revealed no abnormalities, and a urine analysis showed no crystals or blood. Upon questioning, I learned that the cat's people were at their wit's end, feeling like they had tried "everything in the book!" Ultimately, they never came back to pick up their cat.

As I wrote in my foreword to Dr. Lachman's first book, *Dogs on the Couch*, cases like these serve as examples of how we are punishing and destroying our pets for exhibiting their normal behavioral patterns rather than educating ourselves and other pet owners. We need to understand how our pets think and why they act as they do. This will enable us to set them up in appropriate situations, encourage and reward desirable behaviors, and eliminate undesirable behaviors without violence.

This is Dr. Larry Lachman's approach. My staff and I have worked with him in situations such as these for the past twelve years, including the training of our own pets. We have discovered how our pets learn best and then how to put them in sitautions in which they cannot help but succeed. Working with Dr. Lachman has also enabled us to help our clients reward their own animals' small successes with praise and affection, gradually watching the small successes blossom into new and desirable habits.

Again, even the most enlightened approach cannot succeed without the diligent participation of the pet's person. This is one of the biggest frustrations for veterinarians and trainers alike. However, with Dr. Lachman's unique family-systems-therapy approach to cat behavior problems, this pitfall can be avoided, which increases the chance of a successful treatment outcome.

So I invite you to read on and experience a more gentle approach that will make your cats more enjoyable members of your household. Then share your experiences with others. As I have written before, by working together to educate pet owners everywhere, we can stop the needless waste of all those pets that never get a fair chance to fit into someone's family.

INTRODUCTION

Even before our first book, *Dogs on the Couch: Behavior Therapy for Training and Caring for Your Dog,* was published, people who knew we were writing it asked us, "When are you going to do one on cats?" It wasn't so much a polite inquiry, it seemed, as it was a plea for help. "As soon we can," we promised. "Hang in there!" And when *Dogs on the Couch* was finally published in 1999, the pleas became even more persistent; we heard them at book signings and lectures, in e-mails, and in everyday conversation. Who would have thought cats needed "behavior therapy," "family systems" therapy, perhaps even their own version of "puppy Prozac"—some of the things we wrote about in our book about dogs? After all, they're cats! They are supposed to be individualists and nonconformists. It's part of their charm.

But cats are no less prone to behavior problems or a need for some basic training than are dogs, even though people seem more willing to forgive felines their faults. In fact, there are now more cats in the United States than dogs (about sixty million cats *versus* fifty-two million dogs), hence, more cat-behavior problems out there waiting to be solved! And while most of Larry's in-home consults deal with canines, about 60 percent of the e-mails he receives are from cat owners with problems. Here is a typical one:

Dear Dr. Lachman,

My wife and I live in my parents' house in the upstairs. We have a female (spayed) cat, Leisha, which is about 5 to 6 years old now. We got her as a kitten. She was a stray left downtown in front of our neighborhood supermarket in a cardboard box with two siblings. She seemed like such a lovable kitten until just in the last few years my parents got a male kitten (Smokey), which is also now fully grown. Smokey is not neutered, and he comes upstairs and invades her territory quite often. Leisha's food bowl is kept in the upstairs bathroom, and when she goes in to eat she is always anticipating him and growls when she thinks he's around. Sometimes, he is there right by the door and she hisses at him ferociously. Smokey just lies there and stares without a flinch, and never retaliates. Lately she has become quite vicious and unpredictable.

My wife went to pet her just the other morning and the cat began to lick her hand, then suddenly she grabbed my wife's hand with her front paws, bit her, and kicked violently with her hind paws scratching up her arm, leaving deep welts. We don't want to have to get rid of her, and certainly will try almost anything that will stop this aggression.

What advice can you offer, and thank you for your help,

Sincerely,
Ted R.

There *are* fewer specific problems with cats than with dogs. Cats, for example, generally don't tear up the backyard landscaping. And cats, generally, don't suffer from separation anxiety—prolonged separation from their owners—the way dogs do. But cats do have problems. The top three problems Larry's cat clients have are: spray marking instead of using the litter box, destructive clawing, and aggression. (With dogs, the top three problems are housebreaking, separation anxiety, and aggression.)

We focus this book on the six areas that encompass about 98 percent of cat owners' problems:

- housebreaking
- spraying or marking the home
- destructiveness
- the relationship between the cat and other pets in the home
- chronic meowing
- aggression

Dogs on the Couch was considered a groundbreaking book because it was the first one to apply to dogs certain theories and behavior therapy techniques used with humans—techniques Larry has employed in his twenty-four years as a counselor and therapist to humans. Fans of *Dogs on the Couch* will notice that many of the techniques and theories don't change when switching the attention from dogs to cats. For example, consistency of training by all the humans in the household—what human therapists call "family systems therapy"—is critical. The principle of positive reinforcement and the emphasis on nonviolent training and behavior-correcting techniques are also critical. The theories and techniques are merely altered to make them specific to the special problems cats have and to account for the feline psyche.

Cats, being cats, are sometimes more of a challenge to train and require a bit more patience than dogs. The treatment plan for a dog with a specific behavior problem often requires several modifications along the way but usually takes just six to eight weeks to successfully implement. While the behavior-modification plan for a cat usually requires less tweaking and is more straightforward, because a cat does not seem to be as dependent on—or is completely independent from—the owners, it usually takes twice as long to produce consistent results, about twelve to sixteen weeks. But hang in there! Cats can live more than twenty years; we're in this for the long haul, right?

Beyond the "fix-it" aspect of this book, you'll find some of the rich history, philosophy, and even whimsy that the subject of cats evokes. You'll see we knock down some stereotypes.

For example, you'll read in the short case histories that precede each chapter (real cases from Larry's "secret files," with names changed to protect the innocent!) that rather than being aloof and unaffectionate, the majority of his cat clients are very, ahem, "doglike." They come up and greet him when he enters the home, they seek petting and affection, they "speak," and they respond to positive-reward training techniques. Even with "problem" feline clients, rare is the cat that runs and hides and avoids all human contact.

We also uncover the cause of cat phobias, or ailurophobia, in people, and outline the recommended therapeutic intervention for it. We address some of the historical myths about cats, and how the remnants of those myths, or archetypes, influence cat lovers and cat haters alike. By utilizing Carl Jung's theories of personality types and his concept of the masculine-feminine duality—the anima and the animus—we explain from a human psychology vantage point why some people are attracted to cats and make great cat people and why others do not—or why they may even dislike cats altogether.

And for something totally different and intriguing, we conclude with a look at anpsi—animal "ESP"—and explore how the cat, more than any other animal, has been traditionally imbued with this special sixth sense. We also list our favorite cat web sites on the Internet and a sampling of cat-related organizations.

One of the reasons we wrote *Dogs on the Couch* was to cut down on the number of dogs euthanized because their owners believed they couldn't make them behave. That is certainly a primary motivation with this book as well. But, as with *Dogs . . .* , underlying that is a desire to help people better understand and relate to their pets and to help make pet ownership more enriching for humans and animals. As we like to say, by learning more about your pet, you will learn more about yourself.

So, sit back, pull up the ottoman, spread out some catnip—

along with some kitty treats, such as Pounce, Ping-Pong balls, and wand toys—and enjoy a positive, loving, and fun journey into the mind and behavior of the cat.

—*Larry Lachman*
Carmel, California

—*Frank Mickadeit*
Rancho Santa Margarita,
California

February 2000

CATS ON THE COUNTER

CHAPTER 1

THE FREUDIAN FELINE AND FAMILY THERAPY

The Personalities of Cats and
Their Humans

There is no evidence that at any time during its history the cat's
way of life and its reception into human homesteads were purposely
planned and directed by humans, as was the case with all other
domestic animals, at least from a very early stage of their association.
. . . In other words there was no agent domesticating the cat besides
the cat himself.   —Paul Leyhausen

The cat is the only animal which accepts the comforts but rejects the
bondage of domesticity.   —Georges, Comte de Buffon

I usually can tell a great deal about a behavior problem by the
way an owner describes his or her cat. Men, for instance,
sometimes use words like "sneaky," "spiteful," "cunning,"
"wicked," and "ruthless" to describe a misbehaving feline.
Women have used words or phrases like "aggressive," "nasty,"
and "treats me like a play toy" when discussing their male
problem cat. What's going on here? Are these really psycho
kitties from hell? Do cats really exhibit humanlike qualities, or
is something else at work? Some people just seem to click better
than others with cats. Why is that? What personality characteristics should a prospective cat owner have that will ensure a
good feline-person match?

   To foster positive, happy, and healthy relationships between
cats and their human families, we need to address the person-

alities of the cat *and* the human members of the household. As we discussed in our book *Dogs on the Couch,* developing a good person-pet match means taking a thorough inventory of your own personality and temperament. Are you an outgoing, gregarious, constantly-in-motion person? Or are you more private and inwardly focused, someone who enjoys his quiet time? Are you assertive or passive, independent or needy? These questions are crucial in starting and maintaining a positive relationship with your cat.

In a few cases I've seen, an owner ends up with a pet whose personality clashes with his own. No matter what behavior-therapy techniques we might try, things don't work out. The gulf between the owner's temperament and the cat's is too great. These, uh, cat fights almost always end up with the pet being adopted out, abandoned, or euthanized. Fortunately, most cat behavior problems can be solved—if we change not only the cat's behavior but the human's, too.

THE ANIMA AND ANIMUS MEET MORRIS

By using certain theories of personality, we can identify specific characteristics that can increase the success of a person-cat match and avoid unnecessary cat relinquishment by the owner. I've found the most useful theories come from Carl Jung. Born in Switzerland in 1875, Jung was a protégé of Freud until he developed his own approach to psychotherapy called analytic psychology.

Jung believed that both men and women have within their psyches, or personalities, some complementary aspect of the opposite sex's archetype, a universally held image rooted deep in our unconscious. The man has his feminine side, called the anima (a Latin name for female soul-image), which can cause him to have a heightened sense of intuition, sentimental feelings, "irrationality," and other so-called feminine qualities. Some men repress these qualities because they're not "manly."

The woman has a masculine side, or animus (male soul-image), that leads to dogmatic or "rigid" thoughts and opinions but can also be a source of courage, strength, and aggressiveness that she can draw on in a time of need. Women, too, can repress their aggressiveness and other perceived masculine traits for fear of not appearing "ladylike."

In men, the anima helps to balance their psyches so their thoughts, emotions, and behaviors don't go to extremes, leading to overly "macho" acting out or aggression. The animus in women balances their psyches so they, too, don't go to extremes, leading to utter passivity or withdrawal. When it comes to cats, people will often project onto the animal their own image of the opposite gender influence, an image that may have been repressed into their unconscious: men typically project their feminine side, and women project their masculine soul-image.

Projection, a psychological defense mechanism, *shifts* the

cause of anxiety or unpleasant impulses to an external source rather than acknowledging that the anxiety and impulse is coming from within. It's like saying, "The cat hates me," rather than, "I hate the cat."

Many cat aggression or biting cases often involve single women who have a young male cat that is stalking, play biting, or scratching the owner. Frequently, the owner's animus or internalized masculine side leads her to describe the offending cat as being "like a typical male," who is "aggressive," "nasty," "has no respect," and "does his own thing." Some of these women may have unresolved hostility toward men that they are projecting onto their cat. Women cat owners who have a positive internalized masculine archetype tend to describe their male cats as "playful, affectionate, loyal, brave, and energetic." The same theory of projection hold for men. A man with a positive anima will describe his female cat as "sleek, sophisticated, dignified, and affectionate." A man with a negative feminine side who may have unresolved hostility toward women will describe his feline as a "conniving" and "untrustworthy" witch!

When dealing with a case that involves an anima/animus-related problem, I use structural family systems therapy to "reframe" or alter the owner's perception of the meaning behind their cat's behavior problem—including confronting a negative projected anima or animus archetype. If I am not successful in doing this, the plan to alter the cat's misbehavior usually fails. We'll describe those techniques in detail in later chapters.

CODEPENDENT VERSUS INTERDEPENDENT: WHY SOME PEOPLE "CLICK" WITH CATS

One of my favorite descriptions of the difference between cats and dogs comes from the noted veterinarian and author Michael Fox, who writes that dogs are extremely dependent animals and that this almost "pathological dependency" makes them ideal child substitutes. Compared to dogs, the cat is a relatively solitary animal, free from the pressures of needing to join a social group. As Fox says, "Those [people] with strength, courage, and conviction to walk alone—like the cat—often find happiness and fulfillment in their lives. They are not dependent on the views or acceptance of others . . . Man is caught in the double bind of being, like the cat, highly individualistic, but at the same time a social animal with acquired needs."

Cats have not been domesticated to the same degree of dependence as have dogs. The dog has been domesticated for 14,000 years compared to the cat's 3,500. In that time, the cat has really changed very little. Most scientists agree that the small wild cats of Europe, Africa, and the Middle East are the immediate ancestors of the modern domestic cat.

The term *co-dependent* was originally used to describe a person whose life had become unmanageable as a result of living with someone who was an alcoholic or drug user. However, it's now recognized that co-dependent also describes unhealthy behavior patterns that can emerge from a relationship that may *not* involve substance abuse. A co-dependent person is someone who lets another's behavior affect him or her, and who is obsessed with controlling that person's behavior. This definition also fits the majority of men I have counseled who were accused of committing acts of domestic violence against spouses or girlfriends.

All relationships are inherently co-dependent to some degree or another, but when a person operates *primarily* from a co-dependent stance in his relationship, it's cause for concern. This extreme social stance can lead to major conflicts to erupt, not only between humans, but between a cat and its person.

People with extreme co-dependency

- often say yes when they mean no;
- do things they really don't want to do;
- do more than their fair share of the work;
- do things other people are capable of doing for themselves;

- find it easier to feel and express anger about injustices done to others than about injustices done to themselves;
- feel bored, empty, and worthless if they don't have a crisis in their lives, a problem to solve, or someone to help;
- overcommit;
- feel guilty about spending money on themselves or doing unnecessary or fun things for themselves;
- have an extreme fear of rejection;
- look to relationships to provide *all* their good feelings;
- keep letting people hurt them;
- stay in relationships that don't work.

To stop being overly co-dependent, one needs to start meeting his or her own needs and wants. One has to develop self-reliance, self-respect, and self-love. In short, one needs to become more interdependent and self-sufficient.

Self-reliant. Not needy. Sounds very "catlike," doesn't it?

Human beings who are interdependent tend to have the following characteristics:

- the desire and room to grow and explore;
- separate interests of one's own;
- a preservation of mutual integrity;
- a willingness to risk and be real;
- the ability to set functional boundaries;
- the ability to enjoy being alone.

Asserting one's independence does not mean taking the extreme stance of anti-dependency, or radical independence. Some people believe they can take care of themselves entirely, that they need nobody else to fulfill their emotional or social needs. They become unable or unwilling to accept help or guidance from someone else. Their anthem might be "I am a rock. I am an island." But when they encounter an emotional need they can't satisfy on their own, that rock can crumble.

THE DOMESTIC CAT:
THE EPITOME OF INTERDEPENDENCE

The cat is a living, breathing role model of the perfect balance and harmony of both the anima and animus—feminine and masculine—and of the balance between co-dependency and radical independence. A cat has the ability to meet some of its emotional and social needs on its own while satisfying other needs by interacting with its human caretakers. Cats set efficient functional boundaries. Cats keep people from coming into their personal space and allow themselves and their "person" to embody a sense of who they are, distinct and separate from the identity or needs of the other. It's part of the feline mystique. Ever hear cat lovers say that they prefer cats to canines because they're not as "needy" as dogs, that cats do like to give and receive affection, but only when and where they want it, and on their terms? For a cat, co-existing with its people is a true balancing act.

That's why people who achieve a balanced, or interdependent, lifestyle will be most attracted to, and satisfied with, their interactions with cats. For them, interacting with or "owning" a cat can be immensely rewarding and fulfilling! Because the cat is inherently interdependent and balanced in its anima/ animus, it will enable and support the interdependent social stance of its person.

I think this explains why surveys show that single adults over thirty-five and "middle parents"—heads of households under age forty-five who have children under age six—own more cats in the United States than other demographic groups. The thirty-five- to forty-year-old is trying to achieve a balance between intimacy and isolation. Similarly, the middle-parent household typically is made up of people who are trying to move forward as opposed to stagnating and withdrawing from life. Both are very complementary characteristics for a cat person to have. Both groups epitomize the balanced social stance of interdependence and characteristically avoid falling into either the overly dependent or the overly aloof extremes.

Those who have imbalance in their anima or animus, or who project rigid and negative gender characteristics onto the cat, will end up resenting and despising the cat altogether. Someone who is co-dependent will not bond or mesh well with the cat because he or she won't feel sufficiently needed and wanted. The radically independent person who claims to require nothing of anyone will resent even the minimal tasks required of cat care, such as cleaning out litter boxes, providing enough play stimulation, and keeping up with yearly vaccinations.

Moving away from black-and-white, either-or thinking and toward a balanced, shades-of-gray perspective is one way a person can transform from being co-dependent to becoming more interdependent and self-sufficient. An honest assessment of your own anima/animus issues is crucial if you are trying to decide whether a cat will be a good family member for you.

SHOULD YOU OWN A CAT?
TEST YOUR PERSONALITY

When selecting the right animal for you, it's also important to inventory your own likes and dislikes and fundamental temperament. Jung believed there are four main types of human personality:

- Thinking
- Feeling
- Sensation
- Intuition

The "thinking" person is dominated by rational measurements and empirical knowing. They trust the facts. A "sensation" type relies primarily on his or her senses to understand the world around them instead of allowing imagination to color their perceptions. By comparison, the "intuitive" type sees possibilities; they have a perception of reality not known to consciousness, but tapped from the deep reservoirs of the unconscious. They trust their hunches. Often, they're the poets and visionaries of the world. A "feeling" person judges or values the atmosphere and acts accordingly. Because of their empathy, they're good in situations in which personal relationships matter. They also tend to make the best therapists. Most people typically do not rely on just one function, but one type does tend to dominate the way they orient themselves to the world.

Jung's four core types formed the basis of two methods for evaluating personalities—The Myers-Briggs Type Indicator and a condensed version developed in 1978 by psychology professor David Keirsey. Keirsey detailed four base temperament types:

- **Sensation/Perceiving (SP) type.** This person is characterized by the need to be free. She is impulsive and yearns for action.
- **Sensation/Judging (SJ) type.** This person is characterized by the need to be useful to society, to feel he belongs, to perform well. He is obligated to work duties.
- **Intuitive/Thinking (NT) type.** This person is characterized by the need to be competent, and to understand and control nature.
- **Intuitive/Feeling (NF) type.** This person has the need to be authentic, to search for self, and to reach her highest potential.

Unsure which temperament type describes you best? Take the Myers-Briggs Type Indicator or the Keirsey Temperament Sorter test. The Temperament Sorter is available in Keirsey's book *Please Understand Me* or on the Internet at www.keirsey.com.

MATCHING YOUR PERSONALITY TYPE
WITH THE CAT'S

Because they're interdependent, self-sufficient, and freedom-seeking, the Intuitive/Feeling and Sensation/Perceiving types are generally best suited to be cat owners. The cat, by its nature, is very much a combination of both the Intuitive/Feeling and the Sensation/Perceiving personality type.

Those, however, who require control or structure and the need to feel needed and appreciated for social work and acts of giving, as the Intuitive/Thinking and Sensation/Judging personalities frequently are, may be closer to the co-dependent end of the dependency spectrum. This suggests the cat is probably not the best choice of pet for them. Frustration, disappointment, and resentment are likely if an Intuitive/Thinking or Sensation/Judging person gets a cat. The cat's semi-wild, nondependent nature can lead the Intuitive/Thinking or Sensation/Judging person to feel rejected, unappreciated, and unloved by their very interdependent cat.

TREATING THE WHOLE FAMILY

Most of my cat consults involve cats and their people who *are* well matched in interdependency but who are experiencing a recurring behavior problem leading to distress in the household.

About 75 percent of my in-home behavior consultations involve a cat and its Intuitive/Feeling or Sensation/Perceiving owner, who is having difficulty working out behavior problems involving house soiling, spray/marking, clawing/destruction, fighting with other cats, excessive meowing, or aggression toward humans. Only a quarter of my cases involve a true personality mismatch; an inherently Intuitive Feeling/Sensation/Perceiving interdependent cat paired with an Intuitive/Thinking or Sensation/Judging co-dependent–oriented person. In these cases, if we can't work things out by bringing the two parties closer together through compromise, by stretching their predisposed personality characteristics to accommodate each other, then the cat often needs to be placed in another home.

But since most cat behavior cases involve owners whose personalities are well-matched with their cats, you might wonder, Why is there a problem? It's usually because the emotional boundaries between the compatible cat and its person are either too enmeshed (intertwined) or too disengaged (overly rigid with insufficient nurturing and interaction between cat and owner). Therefore, you can't only focus on the cat when working on a severe cat-behavior problem. The owners also must change the way they relate to their cat. The structure and emotional boundaries of the humans and felines must be redefined and enforced. The method by which we do this is called structural family therapy.

This concept was first outlined by family therapist Salvador Minuchin, who believed that the way every person in a family interacts with one another affects the behavior of each family member. To change one person's behavior, each person in the family must change their behavior as well.

A HUMAN EXAMPLE

In 1981, I was counseling a family of three: a single father in his fifties and two daughters, ages fourteen and fifteen. The family entered therapy because the older daughter was stealing, disrupting the classroom, and ditching school. I soon discovered that when attention was focused on the older girl as the "identified patient" and her behavior improved, one of the other family members would begin to act out or deteriorate psychologically. Her younger sister began engaging in autistic-like behavior by banging her head against the wall and floor. She also developed an array of psychosomatic stomach complaints that proved unsubstantiated by medical examination.

I shifted the focus of therapy to the younger girl. Once she improved, and both girls were doing reasonably well, the father lapsed into a deep depression requiring psychiatric medication. New symptoms were cropping up with one family member every time another member began to get attention or started to improve. What was happening?

At the urging of the counseling center's clinical director, I began to apply a structural family therapy model to find the answer. It became apparent that this family was unable to function or to remain stable without one of its members acting out. They lacked the tools to openly discuss negative emotions and solve problems. Instead, they indirectly manipulated one another's behavior by developing symptoms of mental illness. If one of the girls felt depressed and wanted more attention from Dad, instead of saying so, she would either get in trouble in school or display bizarre self-destructive behavior.

At the root of the problem were issues of appropriate boundaries and the ways the family members related to one another. The father had unknowingly crossed the generational boundaries or power structure in the family by inadvertently elevating his eldest daughter to the status of surrogate wife and mother. He did this by coming to her with his problems and asking her to parent her younger sister. The father was too enmeshed with the older girl and too disengaged from the younger one. By altering the way the entire family functioned and related to one another, it was possible to make a lasting change in the original patient.

APPLYING STRUCTURAL FAMILY THERAPY TO CATS

When treating cat-behavior problems, I have found that cat separation anxiety and aggression or biting the owner is rampant in families in which the emotional boundaries are too enmeshed. In cases in which the cat exhibits house soiling, spray/marking, constant meowing, or self-mutilation, the emotional boundaries in the family usually are too disengaged, or rigid. The goal of the animal behaviorist is to change the family system by restructuring the human's emotional boundaries with the cat's, eliminating dysfunctional relationships.

Among other things, structural family therapy is characterized by:

- Assessing the dysfunctional behavior patterns within the family.
- Focusing on altering behavior.
- Rewarding good behavior through positive reinforcement.
- Being brief. Most cat-behavior problems can be remedied within sixteen weeks.
- Being direct. Outline the problem (and solution) for all human family members and tackle it head-on.
- Being gentle. There's never any reason to cause an animal physical pain.

Beginning with chapter 3, we'll describe how to apply these concepts to a variety of cat-behavior problems and bring cat and person closer to the ideal interdependent relationship characterized by a true balance in the masculine-feminine (or animus-anima) natures of both species.

CHAPTER 2

THE FICTIONAL FELINE

Common Cat Myths

The vanity of man revolts from the serene indifference of the cat.
—Agnes Repplier

Kiss the black cat,
And that'll make ye fat:
Kiss the white cat,
And that'll make ye lean.
—Sir John Denham

Every year in October, an edict is issued at animal shelters around the United States: no black cats are to be adopted out until after the thirty-first. Why? Because shelter workers have found that some sickos like to take the cats and kill them at Halloween in ritualistic sacrifices.

The myth of black cats being evil or bad luck goes back at least to the Middle Ages, when it was linked to witchcraft. And of course, everybody from Hollywood to Madison Avenue to the storytime lady at your public library continues to perpetuate the connection. While most people come to know better as they mature, some kids grow up thinking it's okay to be cruel to black cats. Some percentage of these will extend this "license to kill" to all cats, and a small percentage of those people will extend it to humans. An exaggeration? Well, as one of our friends—a vaunted FBI profiler—will tell you, one of the classic trademarks of serial killers is that they tortured and killed small animals as children.

Of course, this is the extreme end of the spectrum. But there are plenty of people out there who just don't like cats or at least are uncomfortable around them. Knowing a bit about the mythology and history of the cat will not only help you understand cats in general, but may help you understand your own feline.

HISTORICAL MYTHS ABOUT CATS

The cat seen as a mysterious, powerful, and often evil force in nature goes back almost as far as recorded history. In Egyptian mythology, the cat symbolized both light and dark, and had an incarnation as both a masculine and feminine deity (echoes of anima and animus) in the forms of the sun god Ra and the maternity goddess Bastet, or Bast. In Roman mythology Diana, the goddess of the hunt, transforms into a cat.

From time to time, the cat gained public favor for a generation or two—perhaps most notably during the height of the Black Plague in the fourteenth century, when they were highly valued in Europe and Asia for killing the rats that were carrying the disease.

But in the fifteenth century, Pope Innocent VIII encouraged the destruction of cats in his attempt to eliminate the practice of witchcraft. Witch-hunting frequently became synonymous with cat-hunting. Cats were burned and drowned, sometimes along with their owners who were accused of being witches. The cat once again became a symbol of evil and not a good thing to have wandering around your garden if you valued your life. And although cats did enjoy brief spurts in popularity, there continued to be a prejudice against the domestic feline to a degree unknown to its canine counterpart, the dog.

It hasn't helped that throughout history many prominent

and influential men were notorious cat-haters, among them William Shakespeare, Johannes Brahms, Louis XIV, and Dwight Eisenhower. History has shown us that what man can't understand or conquer, he will often vilify. Man's reaction to his puzzlement and frustration over not being able to fully domesticate the cat is a good example. Until recently men were the writers of history and the chief purveyors of public opinion, so it's not surprising that many of the lingering negative images of the cat have the feminine tone described in chapter 1.

American men still prefer dogs to cats, according to statistics, but interestingly, the increasing role of women in American public life has led to a recent surge in the cat's popularity. With more women absent from the home during the day and no longer able to care for the relatively "needy" dog, the more self-reliant cat in the late 1990s for the first time overtook the dog as the most common pet in America.

CAT MYTHS TODAY

For the most part, thank goodness, society now realizes that the link between cats and evil is pure nonsense. But a lot of other myths remain. Here are some culled from the American Animal Hospital Association, the Cat Fanciers' Association, and our own experiences.

MYTH: Cats don't like humans.
FACT: Cats do not show their affection the same way dogs do, but they *are* affectionate, and frequently will follow you from room to room or curl up in your lap for some purr-inducing petting. The notion of cats being unfriendly might come from owners responding to the change in behavior they witness as their cats mature. Kittens are very affectionate and cuddly because to survive they have to remain close to their mothers. When they are taken away from their mother, the human be-

comes its surrogate mother. However, as the kitten reaches adolescence, it will become increasingly less dependent on humans for its survival and seek out its person less frequently. It's nothing against humans—it would act the same way toward its biological mother.

MYTH: Cats are mean.
FACT: This fallacy often stems from cats biting their owners after the owners inadvertently overstimulate the cat through excessive petting or grooming. We discuss this type of cat aggression and what to do about it in chapter 6.

MYTH: Cats are lazy.
FACT: In the wild, the cat is a nocturnal hunter, which means it must rest during the day to prepare for the arduous nightly search for food. Domestication hasn't changed that characteristic, even though its "hunt" now consists of meowing until you open its can of tuna. (It's true, however, that this feline trait can be annoying when it sets a cat and its owner on opposite circadian rhythm cycles. The cat might be extremely active at night when the owner is trying to sleep.)

Stephen and Valerie Biggs

MYTH: Cats always land on their feet.
FACT: While cats instinctively fall feet first and might survive falls from high places, they also may break bones in the process. Some kind of screening on balconies and windows can help protect pets from disastrous falls.

MYTH: Cats should drink milk.
FACT: Most cats like milk, but do not need it if properly nourished. Also, they might get diarrhea if they drink too much. If given at all, the amount should be small and infrequent.

MYTH: Cats that are spayed or neutered automatically gain weight.
FACT: Like people, cats gain weight from eating too much, not exercising enough, or both. In many cases, spaying or neutering is done at an age when the animal's metabolism already has slowed, and its need for food has decreased. If the cat continues to eat the same amount, it might gain weight. Cat owners can help their cats stay fit by providing exercise and not overfeeding them.

MYTH: Indoor cats cannot get diseases.
FACT: Cats still are exposed to organisms that are carried through the air or brought in on an owner's shoes or clothing. Even the most housebound cat ventures outdoors at some point and can be exposed to diseases and worms through contact with other animals' feces.

MYTH: Pregnant women should not own cats.
FACT: Some cats can be infected with a disease called toxoplasmosis, which occasionally can be spread to humans through cat litter boxes and cause serious problems to unborn babies. However, these problems can be controlled if the expectant mother avoids contact with the litter box and assigns daily cleaning to a friend or other family member.

MYTH: Cats interfere when you talk on the telephone because they are jealous.
FACT: The cat merely sees and hears its person in the room talking out loud when no other human is present. The cat concludes the owner is talking to it and responds by moving close and rubbing against its person with its head and muzzle.

MYTH: Cats are finicky eaters.

FACT: Cats are carnivores and therefore have little interest in the leaf of lettuce you offer it from your salad. This is not the cat being finicky, which suggests some kind of humanlike desire to be disagreeable. It's merely a dietary condition developed over millennia of evolution. Other reasons for a lack of appetite: cats prefer to eat many small snacklike meals each day rather than one big feast; female cats going into heat sometimes lose their appetites for twenty-four hours or more; your good-intentioned neighbors may be feeding your cat.

MYTH: Tomcats regularly and systematically kill kittens.

FACT: Tomcats have been known to actively participate in the rearing of kittens, providing food and defending the litter against invading humans. Tomcats may, however, be driven away by the mother or simply will ignore the litter. If a tom does kill a kitten, it is frequently as a result of accidentally biting too hard around the kitten's neck when the tomcat is sexually aroused and attempts to mount the kitten.

More myths and factual responses can be found on the Web sites www.healthypet.com and www.cfainc.org.

MYTHS AND STEREOTYPES: SUGGESTIONS FOR CHANGE

Prejudice is an attitude, usually negative, toward a person (or animal) based on his or her membership in a particular group. (I hate cats. Bubba is a cat. Therefore, I hate Bubba.) A stereotype is a social belief that incorporates both positive and negative characteristics supposedly shared by almost all members of a particular group. (Cats are mean. Therefore, Bubba is mean.)

Such attitudes often develop in childhood through one's parents or other adult authority figures. The influential adults might simply pass on negative folklore about cats, or they might display overt hatred for cats by verbally or physically abusing them. These types of modeling behaviors are called, respectively, *information transmission* and *vicarious reinforcement*, and are responsible for many types of prejudice and phobias.

Frequently, prejudice and stereotyping create a self-fulfilling prophecy. The person acts toward cats as if he expects them to be mean or unfriendly. The extremely intuitive cat senses a threat or hostility, triggering in it the very behavior—biting, clawing, or flight—the human is expecting.

To prevent or correct prejudice and negative stereotypes about cats, four things are important:

EARLY EDUCATION: Children should be given the facts about cats at home and in school. When stories are read to them in which cats are portrayed as evil, cunning or dangerous, children should be told that in real life the average housecat is none of those things.

CRITICAL THINKING: This means not blindly accepting the party line, but going out in the world, researching and discovering the truth for oneself. This is only accomplished by rejecting a worldview in which all things are black or white, and by being open to exceptions to whatever global generalizations one has been exposed to while growing up. Children should be encouraged to use their cognitive reasoning skills as early as they are able.

EMPATHY: Try to understand a cat's behavior from its point of view. When a cat is scratching the furniture, bringing home dead birds, or "bothering" you when you are on the phone, stop for a minute and try to think about what's behind this behavior using the information contained in this book. Is there another possible meaning or interpretation? If so, how does that affect your emotional reaction and stereotyping of the cat?

When empathy and tolerance are increased, prejudice and negative stereotypes decrease.

FREQUENT CONTACT WITH CATS: It's hard to hold on to negative stereotypes if a person has regular social contact with a number of cats in a variety of settings and sees the differences in personality and the affection, loyalty, and devotion cats exhibit toward people. More and more accumulated "exceptions" will ultimately disprove the stereotype. If there are children in your neighborhood who don't have cats, ask their parents if you can introduce them to your cat and allow them to pet it and even feed it.

By being aware of the origins of negative myths regarding the cat, and implementing the above strategies to overcome them, we should be able to reduce the numbers of cats in this country that are abused, euthanized, or relinquished by their owners.

CHAPTER 3

GOOD HOUSEKEEPING

Introducing Cats to New Homes

*I love cats because I enjoy my home, and little by little, they become
its visible soul.*
　　　　　　　　　　　　　　　　　　　—Jean Cocteau

Never quite fulfilled is the household without a cat or two.
　　　　　　　　　　　　　　　　—Rogers E. M. Whitaker

FROM LARRY'S CASE FILES:

CASE 1
FILE # 98-03314
CAT'S NAME: Lacey
BREED: Domestic shorthair
AGE: Two years
PROBLEM: House soiling after moving into a new home

In September of 1998, I went out on a consultation involving a
spayed female shorthair, "Lacey," that had begun to urinate outside of her litter box after her family had moved into a new
home. This had been going on for about eight months. She first
began to have accidents in the kitchen, then in the bathroom
near the shower, then in the upstairs hallway. Lacey was now
confined to the laundry room. She was a healthy cat, obtained
when she was eight weeks old from a neighbor whose cat had

had a litter of kittens. Besides being spayed at six months of age, Lacey had not undergone any major surgery. A veterinarian had put Lacey on the anti-anxiety drug Valium to stop her house soiling. It worked temporarily, but as soon as they began to wean Lacey off the Valium, the accidents began again. That's when the veterinarian referred Lacey and her people to me.

CASE 2
FILE # 96-08841
CATS' NAMES: Ted and Tapu
BREED: Domestic shorthairs
AGES: Six years
PROBLEM: Sibling cat fighting after moving into a new home

In April of 1996, I went out on a consult involving two cats, Ted and Tapu, that were neutered males from the same litter. For more than six years, they were the best of buddies until one year prior to my visit, when Ted and Tapu's owners moved into a new home. Suddenly, both cats acted "spooky" and would "slither" around the house, first avoiding each other, then hissing and growling, and, in the last six months, attacking each other. The owners were distressed. They had tried confining the cats as well as introducing them to each other while one cat was being held by an owner, but nothing worked. The cats would still try to fight. If I couldn't help them through behavior therapy, the owners were going to find one of the cats a new home.

CATS AND THEIR TERRITORY

Cats are *very* attached and attuned to their physical environment. While dogs seem to be more attuned to the people in a particular place rather than the place itself, the reverse is true for cats. Therefore, moving into a new home can be especially traumatic for a cat.

Some veterinarians and other observers of cat behavior believe that staking out and guarding their turf is more important to cats than eating or mating. And any threat to a cat's territory can impact its appetite and social interaction.

When distressed and suffering anxiety because of disruptions in its household, the extroverted cat will tend to vent its distress or frustration onto furnishings in the home—clawing the sofa, tearing up the drapes, urinating on the carpet, etc. It might destroy things that smell of its owners. The more introverted cat will tend to compulsively lick itself, vomit, or experience chronic medical problems. Psychologists call this somaticizing—converting emotional distress into bodily symptoms.

A relaxed, mentally healthy cat will tend to perch and sleep out in the open, frequently on windowsills or shelves. When the cat doesn't feel comfortable, it will seek sanctuary. So when a cat goes through a trauma, such as a change in its environment, it needs a "time-out" place where it can retreat and relax. You can help relieve your cat's anxiety by providing it a comfortable, safe place in the home it can go to and be completely away from children and other pets. If you put in this place a used towel or old shirt you have worn, this will give the cat the comforting scent of its owner.

World renowned cat therapist Carole Wilbourn says that cats are creatures of habit; "their anticipation of routine activities increases their security and happiness." When this "stable-sameness" is disturbed, anxiety is created and a variety of behavior problems can erupt.

ANXIETY TRIGGERS

Going from the highest level of trauma to the lowest, here is a list of specific environmental changes that can cause anxiety in cats:

- moving into a new home
- bringing home a new cat or dog
- introducing into the home a new person, adult, or child
- having temporary workers around the home
- bringing home a new piece of furniture
- building onto the home
- having houseguests
- new pets moving in next door
- changing the home routine
- someone leaving the household
- household disharmony

If these events do indeed cause anxiety, the cat will most often demonstrate it by:

- house soiling and not using the litter box
- spraying or marking walls and furniture
- ceasing to eat
- excessive grooming practices
- excessive meowing
- excessive destructiveness
- becoming aggressive

We address dealing with these specific symptoms of anxiety elsewhere in this book. However, it is most desirable, of course, to prevent the anxiety in the first place by helping your cat adjust to a new environment.

SMOOTHING THE TRANSITION

There are several steps we recommend a cat owner take when introducing a cat to a new home. In general, these work well whether you are introducing a current pet to a new home or a new pet to your existing home.

- Before the actual move—as much as two weeks in advance, if possible—bring items that smell of the new home and place them where the cat is currently sleeping and eating. This will help the cat make a positive association with its new environment and help it get used to the new scent.
- Likewise, rub a towel or blanket on your cat, take it to the cat's future home, and rub it on floors, walls, and furniture. When the cat arrives, it will recognize its own familiar scent and experience less anxiety.
- As much as possible, place the cat's items and toys in the same locations as in its previous home. For example, if your cat ate and drank in the kitchen and had its litter box in the downstairs bathroom, then place the cat's bowls in the kitchen of the new home and its litter box in the bathroom. This will help establish a "stable-sameness."
- If the whole household is moving into a new home, do not bring your cat over until all the hectic moving is done and the movers and guests are gone. Then bring the cat to its new home safely, in a cat carrier that has openings, or little screen doors, on top as well as on one side. Be sure this is not the first time the cat has been in the carrier. (To get the cat used to the carrier, try feeding it in the carrier with the door open a few times before you actually move.)
- Pick one room in the new home that your cat will make its "base camp" for two to four weeks. This can be your bedroom, an upstairs guestroom, or a bathroom. Place its litter box on one end of the room on the floor, and its food and water up high on the opposite end of the room. Spread copious amounts of catnip, catnip-filled toys, kitty treats, and cheese treats around the floor. Include a "kitty condo" and/or scratching post. Your cat should remain in this room until it is showing signs of relaxation and comfort—lying or perching out in the open, seeking you out

and purring, eating on schedule, playing, and being back on its usual litter box schedule.

- After the two- to four-week period, add one new room per week, letting your cat explore—either freely, in a cat carrier, or on leash and harness—the other "far kingdoms" of the home until it exhibits similarly comfortable and nonstressed behaviors in these rooms as well.

- Make sure all windows and doors are closed, and appliances like refrigerators and dishwashers are securely shut.

CATS ON THE COUNTER

As your cat feels more secure in its new surroundings, it may tend to jump up on the kitchen counter, dresser, or mantlepiece. If you do end up with a "cat on the counter," you then must *redirect* your cat to appropriate climbing objects such as kitty condos and floor-to-ceiling cat trees. Hide some catnip, kitty treats, Pounce treats, and some cheese or tuna to induce your cat to use these appropriate items to climb and perch on. When you can't supervise, prevent your cat from gaining access to the off-limits locations to by closing off the kitchen or bedroom.

ADDITIONAL SAFETY CONSIDERATIONS

The Cat Fanciers' Association and the ASPCA's National Animal Poison Control Center offer some tips for a poison-safe household for your cat:

1. Be aware of the plants you have in your house—and in your yard, if your cat will have outside access. (The CFA advocates cats being kept indoors at all times.) The ingestion of azalea, oleander, Easter lily, or yew plant material by a cat could be fatal.

2. Never allow your cat access to the area where cleaning agents are used or stored.
3. When using pesticides such as rodent bait, roach traps, or snail bait, place them in areas inaccessible to your cat.
4. Never give your cat any medications unless under the direction of a veterinarian.
5. Keep all prescription and over-the-counter drugs out of reach of your cat.
6. Never leave chocolates unattended.
7. Before using anti-flea products on your cat or in your household, contact your veterinarian for a specific recommendation for your pet.
8. When using a fogger or a house spray for bugs, make sure to remove your cat from the area for the time period specified on the container.

9. When treating your lawn or garden with fertilizers, herbicides, or insecticides, always keep your cats away from the area until the area is completely dry. Discuss usage of the products with the manufacturer and always store them in an area that will ensure no cat exposure.

CASE STUDIES POSTSCRIPT

Lacey
I outlined the anti–house soiling program detailed in chapter 5 of this book for Lacey and her people. Lacey's owner reported that within the first two weeks the cat's frequency of urination accidents had noticeably subsided. By the end of the initial eight-week period, as we were giving Lacey more and more freedom, her urination accidents ceased altogether and Lacey seemed to be getting more and more relaxed in her new home.

Ted and Tapu
With this battling duo, we used a combination of family therapy, behavior modification intervention, and buspirone (BuSpar) prescribed by a veterinarian. But even with this multilayered plan—anti-anxiety medication, one-on-one daily stress-management sessions, rubbing towels on each cat and exchanging scent, separating them when the owners were out or asleep—it still took a while. At the four-month period, Ted and Tapu finally quit fighting and settled into their new home.

CHAPTER 4

LASSIE MEETS MORRIS/ MORRIS MEETS SIMBA

Introducing Dog to Cat/Cat to Cat

No tame animal has lost less of its native dignity or maintained more of its ancient reserve. The domestic cat might rebel tomorrow. —William Conway, Archbishop of Armagh

Cats don't belong to people. They belong to places. —Wright Morris

FROM LARRY'S CASE FILES:

CASE 1
FILE # 94-90101
DOG'S NAME: Sheila
BREED: Sheltie-Pomeranian mix
CATS' NAMES: Lucky and Mushu
BREEDS: Maine coon and tabby
PROBLEM: Dog-cat conflicts

In 1994, I went out on a behavioral consult regarding a newly acquired one-year-old female Sheltie-Pomeranian. The owner had adopted Sheila from the pound three weeks prior to my visit. There was no history as to how the dog was raised, the personality of its parents, and whether or not the dog was adequately socialized with other animals. The owner picked Sheila because she was the quietest dog at the shelter. When she tried to introduce Sheila to her two cats already in residence, Lucky and Mushu, the dog growled and chased them throughout the house. Both cats were declawed and therefore could not defend themselves.

All three pets were indoor animals, so their owner was forced to set up some baby gates during the day, segregating Sheila downstairs and giving Lucky and Mushu the upstairs, where their litter box and food was located. When Sheila was being aggressive toward Lucky and Mushu, the owner resorted to heavy-handed methods for corrections, such as hitting the dog under its chin with her hand or yanking on its choke chain. This only made Sheila more aggressive and, in my opinion, made the dog associate negative events (being hit and choked) with the presence of the two cats.

If I couldn't help the owner to get these three to get along—or at least tolerate one another without aggression—Sheila was headed back to the pound.

CASE 2
FILE #94-90914
CATS' NAMES: Sammy, Fred, Maple, Kaluha, Margie, and Suki
BREEDS: Blue Point Siamese and domestic shorthairs and longhairs
PROBLEM: Fighting

Also in 1994, I went out on a consultation involving a home with *six* cats. The five-year-old neutered male Blue Point Siamese, Sammy, had begun to spray-mark in the home and fight with three of his five feline housemates: Fred, a seven-year-old neutered male shorthair; Kaluha, a ten-month-old neutered male shorthair; and Suki, a one-year-old spayed female longhair. Sammy either ignored or got along with Maple, a one-year-old neutered male longhair, and Margie, a ten-month-old spayed female shorthair.

The owner had gotten Sammy from a cattery in San Bernardino, California, when he was six weeks old—a little too young to be given away. Sammy's owner wanted a Blue Point Siamese because she had had one when growing up and admired the breed's intelligence and appearance. Sammy used his litter box from the very beginning without any problems. Sammy was friendly toward people and strangers and would frequently jump on their shoulders to literally "hang out." Sammy was neutered and a healthy cat with no history of injuries, disease, or emergency surgeries. When Sammy began spraying and fighting, his owner sought help from a veterinarian, who first put Sammy on Valium, then BuSpar, and then Elavil. Sammy reacted badly to all three medications and none of them had fully stopped either the spray-marking or the aggression. Sammy's owner was now consulting with a holistic veterinarian for possible use of homeopathic remedies such as Valerian root.

When Sammy began his spray-marking eight months prior, he sprayed a planter at the back window, the couch, and most of the perimeter of the home. (See chapter 5, "Feline Fastidiousness and the Turf Cat," for more information on this.) His aggressiveness began when the owner added Kaluha and Suki to the mix. For the other cats' safety and to prevent further furniture damage, the owner banished Sammy to the rear patio. My job: to reintegrate Sammy back into the main part of the house and eliminate his aggressiveness.

CATS AND TERRITORIALITY

Experts believe cats have a home territory and range that are connected by a network of well-delineated pathways, protected by visual contact and displays of dominant behavior. When a new cat is brought into a home where another cat already lives, the resident cat will be dominant by nature of its claim to the preexisting territory. Not only is a trespassing cat inspected and possibly attacked, but familiar cats also scrutinize and sniff one another as if they were strangers. This brings up a very interesting class of cat-to-cat aggression cases that I have seen over the last couple of years.

FELINE REDIRECTED AGGRESSION: WOLFIE AND THE TRESPASSING TOM

Recently, I have encountered several cases of cats that for years have gotten along smashingly only to become aggressive toward one another because of a trespassing cat that cries or spray-marks on the outside of the home. What is happening is that one or all of the inside cats are becoming defensive, agitated, and aggressive about this new intruder and are redirecting this territorial reaction onto one another—or even onto the owner. If unchecked, the aggressiveness among the cats will increase and feline harmony will never return to the home.

One of my consults was at a home made up of *four* cats, all three-year-old Siamese mixes from the same litter: Wolfie and Java, which were males; and Blanca and India, which were females. After a stray tomcat began hanging out on the owner's front porch, Wolfie began spray-marking inside the house and attacking his three sibling cats. Eventually, the three victims, expecting this behavior, began preemptively striking back, causing the owner to segregate Wolfie in the bathroom and to put the other three in another part of the home. This counter-aggression was most frequently demonstrated by Java, the other male.

Some history on Wolfie: He was adopted at six weeks of age from an animal rescue group and was litter-box trained in no time. His owner prepared a daily homemade meal for Wolfie and his cat mates that included salmon, organic vegetables, oats, pumpkin, raw turkey, and vitamin supplements. Wolfie was neutered at six months of age and, other than a recent ear irritation responsive to the homeopathic agent arnica, had been a healthy cat. He used his kitty condo and cat tree. While initially leery toward visitors, he would eventually warm up to them, as he did to me on my first visit.

This case was complicated for several reasons: First, there were four cats, and although Wolfie had been the original instigator of aggression, now all the cats to some degree were aggressive toward him. Second, he was still spraying in the house, even though the tomcat had stopped coming onto the front porch when the owner began using a scent solution called Boundary outside, and the pheromone product Feliway inside the house. And third, with four cats and only one owner, there were some logistical and safety problems implementing the daily "reconditioning" exercises I prescribed.

To solve this last problem, I had the owner work with Wolfie and just one other cat at a time—with Wolfie on leash and harness—during the exercises. These consisted of bringing the cats into the same room and rewarding them with treats and praise for being tolerant and civil when they approached each other. Any aggressiveness was corrected with a time-out or a squirt of water. As the cats showed less aggression and defensiveness, we increased the number of cats present, until all four could be in the same room with no problem.

Because of the seriousness of the aggression, the owner also sought help from her veterinarian, who used both traditional and natural remedies. For two of the cats, "Rescue Remedy" or Valerian root worked fine, and, along with family systems behavior therapy I provided, took the edge off their anxiety and reduced their aggression. For the other two cats, including Wolfie, the vet prescribed the psychotropic drugs Elavil or BuSpar.

About twelve weeks into the program, I received this e-mail update from Wolfie's owner:

Hi, Dr. Larry:
Just wanted to let you know that Wolfie and the other 3 (Java, Blanca and India) are back on track; a rather slow track, but one none the less.

I have found a treat that transcends all fears for Wolfie and Java. It's my honey-cured turkey that I have sliced at the deli. So, that's the ticket for us. I hook everyone up in their harnesses and leashes and I dish out the turkey treats and warm fuzzies. After they have gobbled up a good amount of turkey, we play with the feather fishing pole toy. I have found that they like to pounce on the stick end of the toy while it is under the little front door carpet. They are so into the game that they really don't pay attention to the fact that Wolfie is playing too. I have found that I can get him to participate in this more than anything else. Wolfie has finally stopped trying to get out of his harness and just relaxes if he doesn't want to play.

I have learned a very valuable lesson . . . they are taking much longer than I expected, however, I can see that I probably rushed the process a few times just because they had a couple of good days. I have finally figured out that I would rather take it slow than to end up taking giant steps backwards. Slow is much better for all of us . . .

Because of the number of cats, the frequency of aggression, and having only one person to do all the training, the behavior modification program took about twenty-four weeks to produce consistent results. (In single-cat homes, or when more than one owner is working the plan, about sixteen weeks is the norm.) At my last checkup, things were going well, the overt aggression had stopped and Wolfie's spraying, although not altogether eradicated, had been substantially reduced.

A SECOND CAT

It is important for cat owners to think carefully before adding another cat to the household. A bad match or a traumatic introduction can lead to having to give away one cat or having one injure the other.

If the reason you want to get another cat is to keep your

first cat company, it may not be the best idea. Cats are very territorial and may not react well to an "invasion." Here's one all-to-common scenario: A cat owner fails to give his cat enough attention. The cat experiences anxiety over this lack of attention. It might stop eating, engage in excessive grooming or meowing, or stop consistently using its litter box. As a quick fix, the owner decides to get another cat so he doesn't have to bother giving the first cat more quality time and attention; the new cat will do it for him. *Wrong!*

Introducing a new cat into the home—especially if the original cat is a mature cat and the new cat is the same sex and close in age—can increase the first cat's anxiety to the point that it begins to spray around the house or attack the new cat or the owner. Now the owner has two cats that need more attention.

Cat therapist Carole Wilbourn talks about how she herself made the mistake of rushing the introduction of her two cats, Sam and Oliver. "Unwittingly, I did everything I could to dampen their relationship. I tried to push them together and yelled at Oliver if he struck out at Sam. The more attention I gave Sam, the more alienated Oliver became. It didn't occur to me that Oliver needed my support and that my husband could comfort Sam."

If you are determined to get a second cat, and you have the time, energy, space, and financial wherewithal to pull it off, there are several things you can do to increase the likelihood the new relationship will be a success:

- Get a kitten, preferably the opposite sex of the cat you have now. Have the cat spayed and neutered.
- If looking for a purebred, select the second cat from a breed that has a reputation for easily getting along with .other cats. Some Siamese, Burmese, and Russian blues tend to fight more than Persians, Himalayans, and domestic shorthairs.

- Keep the two cats completely separated for one month. During this period, give your first cat more attention, treats, play sessions, and reassurances, reinforcing its dominance in the home.
- Rub towels on each cat. Then swap the towels, placing them where each cat sleeps and eats. This will help the cats get used to the other's scent and to begin to make a positive association with its new housemate.
- After one month, gradually introduce them to each other. With at least one cat on leash and harness or confined in the cat carrier, let them see and sniff each other, while spreading catnip and treats. Gradually increase the visual space, access, and socialization time. Hissing, batting, and posturing are to be expected initially. However, prevent the cats from chasing or stalking each other, even if it means calling it quits for the day, or backing up the process a step or two and going slower.

There will be a "getting-to-know-you" period of three to six months before the cats arrive at whatever mutually tolerant or positive relationship they are going to have. If after six months, one or both cats are still seriously aggressive, consult your veterinarian about anti-anxiety medication and implement the reconditioning programs outlined later in this chapter.

CATS AND DOGS

When mixing cats and dogs, it's easiest to get the cat first. Let it mature, maintain its claws, and then get the dog, preferably as a puppy. This way, the puppy will grow up being around the cat and see it as a fellow pack member. Also, having each spayed or neutered will lead to a more amicable relationship. Here's how to introduce them:

- Protect the cat's feeding and litter box areas from intrusion by the dog. Feeding the cat in a high location works well.
- When you first bring the puppy home, crate it or put it on a leash so the cat can investigate the dog without being chased or trampled.
- Caress and praise the cat and give it catnip and treats whenever it is around or approaches the contained puppy.
- Then let the dog sniff the cat while it is in the cat carrier. Give the dog petting, praise, and treats when it behaves appropriately around the cat.
- After a month of these structured socialization sessions, gradually give the cat more and more freedom around the dog. Start with the dog being on a short leash or in its crate and work up to having it on a twenty-foot leash. Only after at least one month of consistent, sustained good behavior by both animals should you take the dog off its leash. If there are problems, back up a step or two and start over.

Inge Brown

During this introductory period we strongly suggest non-force obedience training for the dog. See our previous book, *Dogs on the Couch: Behavior Therapy for Training and Caring for Your Dog.*

IF THE INTRODUCTION PROGRAM DOESN'T WORK

If you have tried one of these introduction programs and your cats, or your cat and dog, are still fighting, you need a behavior therapy reconditioning program. You need to switch condition these bad attitudes before the pets will get along.

Preliminary Steps to Correcting Cat-Dog Conflict
- Separate the cat and dog when you aren't home.
- Before reintroducing them in daily socialization sessions, give the dog a week or two of sit-stay practice. Here's what to do:

    1. Put a short leash on the dog. Put the loop handle around your left wrist and have a handful of treats in the left hand.
    2. Have your dog sit in front of you by giving it the sit command with your right hand.
    3. Open your right hand with the palm facing the dog and say "stay."
    4. Almost at the same instant you give the command, take a quick quarter-step to your right, and then immediately step right back to your dog *before it has a chance to move.*
    5. If the dog has remained in the sit, say "good stay," reach into your left hand for a treat, and give the dog the treat with your right hand.
    6. *Immediately,* as the dog is chewing the treat for the previous stay, open your right hand again and give the "stay" command.

7. Keep your right hand open and up as you take another quick quarter step to the right and return to the dog before it gets a chance to move. Reward again. Repeat six to eight times for puppies, ten to fifteen times for older dogs. Do this once a day, three days in a row.

8. Beginning the fourth day of the first week, begin to increase the distance. Take two small steps away from the dog, this time at a forty-five-degree angle from it, and return quickly before it can move away.

9. On the fifth day, take three steps, on the sixth day, four or five steps. At the end of the first week, you should be able to get to the end of the short leash and immediately back to the dog without the dog getting up and following you.

10. Once you have established some distance at the end of the first week, try to get the dog to stay for increasingly longer periods of time. After you give the "stay" command once, repeat it several times as you back away and look at your watch. Start with ten-second stays for a puppy and fifteen-second stays for an older dog. If the dog stays, walk back to it and reward with "good stay" and three treats, given one at a time. Increase the time to twenty seconds for a puppy, thirty seconds for an older dog. If the dog stays, reward it with a "good stay" and four treats. The longer the dog stays, the more treats it gets. Over six to eight weeks you should be able to work up to a daily regimen of three sets of ten sits and a half-hour stay for a mature dog, and three sets of six sits and a five-minute stay for a puppy. For a more thorough sit-stay program, see *Dogs on the Couch*.

- During this time, give the cat one-on-one focus sessions without the dog present. The session should take place in a specific part of the home and include catnip toys, catnip, and gentle caressing.
- Rub a towel on the dog and put it where the cat sleeps and eats and vice versa.
- Don't allow the dog to jump up on furniture.

After completing these preliminary steps for a dog-cat conflict, you can begin the twice-a-day reconditioning "socialization happy hour."

Preliminary Steps to Correcting Cat-Cat Conflict

Begin by having the cats separated and reintroducing them with "sniff" contact underneath a closed door. Give them catnip and treats. Then move to visual contact by cracking open the door an inch and stoppering it so it can't be forced open wider. You also can put them on opposite sides of a window screen. Again give praise and treats. When that goes well (no hissing, growling, or lunging) proceed to the following program.

Second Stage: Dog-Cat or Cat-Cat Conflict Resolution

1. For the duration of this program, only give the pets attention during these sessions. This will reinforce the notion that good things happen *only* when they are together and behaving.
2. Bring the cat into a large room by itself, sit down at the spot farthest from the door, and start its one-on-one catnip session, giving it praise and treats as you dole out the goodies. If you are working with two cats, choose the least aggressive of the two for this role.
3. Have another person bring the dog or the other cat into the room. A dog should be on a leash and an antipull collar. A cat should either be on a leash or in an animal

carrier with a metal mesh door through which it can see the cat that is already in the room. If you are working with a dog, as you approach the cat, have the dog do several sit-stays—every five to ten feet—until it is next to the cat.

4. If the dog breaks its stay, growls, barks, or snaps, blast it in the chest with water and say "Off!" After a five-minute respite, resume the session. If a cat begins to show aggressiveness in its body language (ears flat back, tail quickly swishing, crouching, hissing, etc.), redirect the cat to a positive distraction, like a Ping-Pong ball toss or catnip toy. If this doesn't work and the aggression is escalating, squirt the offending cat and say "Off!" Separate the animals, wait five or ten minutes, and try again. You want to at least get to the point where neither pet is growling, hissing, or striking out at the other.

5. Start with short daily sessions of five minutes so you don't overwhelm the animals and too severely test their tolerance for each other. During the sessions, give both pets copious amounts of attention, petting, playing, and treats. They should gradually become positively conditioned to want to be in each other's presence for increasing lengths of time.

6. As the days go by and incidents of aggressive body language and behavioral displays become fewer, lighten up the restrictions. Take the cat out of the carrier or off the short leash and put it on long leads. Only when they both show consistent signs of being tolerant (if not overjoyed) to be in the presence of their housemate should you allow them to roam freely in the room where the sessions take place.

7. If after a few weeks one (or both) of the animals just doesn't seem to be adjusting and still appears overly anxious in the presence of the other, consult your veterinarian about using an anti-anxiety medication in conjunction with this counter-conditioning program.

After twelve to sixteen weeks of counter-conditioning, the animals should be looking forward to being with their house-mate and there should be no signs of aggression. They should at the very least tolerate each other, and in some cases might become best friends.

A Cautionary Note

This program tends to work best with dogs that are merely undersocialized, as opposed to those that are engaging in pred-atory hunting aggression. In cat-to-cat aggression cases, it works best with cats that *have* been socialized with other cats and are generally friendly, but that are going through a rough transition with the arrival of a "sibling" in the home.

If the situation involves dogs with predatory aggression, cats that were *never* socialized with other cats, or cats that were weaned from their moms and littermates prior to eight weeks of age, the chances of success are not very good. Such dogs and cats would not be amendable to the program out-lined above and should be placed in a single-pet home be-cause the danger to the smaller or less-aggressive animal is very real.

CASE STUDIES POSTSCRIPT

Sheila

A week after my initial visit, the owner reported that things were going well and Sheila was beginning to respond to the program. At the end of two months, Sheila no longer growled and chased the cats, and one of the two cats was beginning to inch closer and closer to Sheila, apparently seeking out a relationship.

Sammy

Two months after my visit with Sammy, Fred, Maple, Ka-luha, Margie, and Suki, the owner reported that the aggression had ceased, although Fred and Suki weren't head-over-heels over Sammy, and that the spray/marking was much better and was well on its way to being completely eradicated. Case closed.

FELINE FASTIDIOUSNESS AND THE "TURF" CAT

Solving Litter Box Problems and Stopping Your Cat from Spraying Indoors

As every cat owner knows, nobody owns a cat.
—Ellen Perry Berkeley

Cats can be very funny, and have the oddest ways of showing they're glad to see you. Rudimace always peed in our shoes.
—W. H. Auden

FROM LARRY'S CASE FILES

CASE 1
FILE #96-04877
CAT'S NAME: Lisette
BREED: White Persian
AGE: Three years
PROBLEM: House soiling

In June of 1996, I was called out to see an affectionate three-year-old White Persian. Lisette had been purchased from a breeder at three months of age and exhibited a sweet disposition, both toward her owner's family and visitors. The owner had selected Lisette because she was so adorable and because she was the last female in the litter. Lisette was an indoor cat that slept on the owner's bed at night and would be rewarded for good behavior through hugs, kisses, and Pounce treats. The problem: Lisette, litter box trained for more than two years, was suddenly defecating in the house every day. She especially liked leaving her little presents in the dining room.

I took down some medical information. Other than being spayed at seven months of age, Lisette had had no surgeries or major illnesses. The veterinarian had ruled out medical problems for the house soiling such as cystitis, Feline Urological Syndrome, and parasites. Because Lisette exhibited no obvious physical problems, I asked her owner about any changes in the family environment. As I suspected, there had been some significant changes in Lisette's life: Her owner had begun to work longer hours and was spending less time with Lisette, the owner's mother was temporarily staying in the home, and Lisette's owner was having some work done to the house, so contractors and their crews were now frequently visiting.

CASE 2

FILE #95-03012
CATS' NAMES: Thomas, Jeeter, and K. C.
BREEDS: Domestic shorthair
AGES: Eleven, five, and four years, respectively
PROBLEM: House soiling

In March of 1995, I went out on an in-home consult involving three domestic shorthairs. The owners had recently moved into the home. At the previous house, K. C. had been sporadically caught urinating on the owners' bed, and this behavior was continuing. With the move into the new home, the two other cats were now getting into the act as well: Jeeter had been caught urinating on the carpet and throw rugs and Thomas had begun defecating near the kitchen table.

Thomas, a black male domestic shorthair, had been adopted from an animal shelter at eight years of age; K. C., a female brindle domestic shorthair, was also adopted from an animal shelter; and Jeeter, a female, lightly spotted domestic shorthair, was found as a stray at about six months of age. All three were spayed or neutered. At night, Thomas would sleep on a downstairs chair, K. C. would sleep on the couch, and Jeeter would sleep in the owners' bedroom. The owners used deodorized clay litter and completely cleaned the home's two litter boxes once every six weeks. Thomas and Jeeter seemed well-adjusted socially, and if not outgoing were at least indifferent to strangers. K. C. was shy, frequently hiding under a bed when a stranger entered the house.

CASE 3

FILE #90-01140
CAT'S NAME: Ninja
BREED: Burmese mix
AGE: Two years
PROBLEM: Spray marking the home

In late 1990, I went out to see a two-year-old male Burmese mix. The owner had gotten Ninja from a neighbor who had a litter of kittens for sale. Ninja was brought home at six weeks of age and had been successfully litter box trained. Ninja had not marked in the owner's previous two homes, but had begun to spray in the new home three weeks prior to my visit. The owner first found evidence of Ninja's spraying on her coat, which was hanging in a closet, and on a banister. The owner had caught Ninja backing up to the banister, shaking his tail, and shooting out a spray of urine before running off. In response, the owner would scream and give chase. Besides being neutered, declawed, and treated for tapeworms, Ninja had been a relatively healthy cat.

LITTER BOX PROBLEMS

A few helpful things to know before we tackle this:

- It is normal for cats to have surface and location preferences for urination and defecation.
- It is a myth that cats don't use the litter box in order to get revenge for something that offended or angered them.
- Cats are not born knowing how to use a litter box. It is something that is learned from their mother and littermates or by owners who help to guide them on the right path through confinement and redirection.
- Some authorities have written that most house soiling problems will clear up on their own within a couple of weeks or months; after whatever is stressing out the cat subsides, the cat will go back to its normal fastidious behavior and regularly use the litter box again. This is contrary to my experience. Without intervention using family systems therapy and behavior modification techniques, the problem usually becomes chronic.

Not using the litter box for either urination or defecation is the single most common problem I see among my cat clients. Sometimes, the cat simply was never completely litter box trained; it was taken from its mother and littermates before it learned how to do it, or the owner stopped the reinforcement behavior before it really imprinted on the cat. Among cats that were adequately trained, about half the time the problem is physical and about half the time it is psychological, or behavioral. The first step with a cat that stops using the litter box is to figure out which category it fits into. Start by having your veterinarian examine your cat. The things you want the vet to check for and rule out are:

1. Cystitis (bladder infection)
2. Feline Lower Urinary Tract Disease (formerly called

Feline Urological Syndrome; also known as "crystals")
3. Parasitic worms
4. Coccidosis/Giardia
5. Impacted anal glands
6. Tumors

If the vet finds one of these problems and successfully treats it, oftentimes the house soiling problem will go away. Also, certain drugs, such as steroidal medication, can cause cats to urinate outside the litter box.

Sometimes, however, even though the original house soiling incidents were prompted by a physical problem, eliminating the physical problem won't eliminate the house soiling. This is because the physical condition has persisted long enough that the house soiling has become a habit for the cat. At that point, the house soiling ceases to be a physical problem and becomes a behavioral one. This scenario represents about half the cat house soiling cases I see.

THE OTHER 50 PERCENT

The other half of my cases involve a cat that either was never quite fully housebroken or successfully litter box trained to begin with, or one that just underwent a significant and emotionally upsetting change in its home environment. This change triggered acute anxiety that was manifested in the form of urinating or defecating outside its litter box. The cat is often urinating or defecating on or near something that smells of its owners—comingling its scent with the owners' to "self-medicate" and reduce anxiety. (Besides house soiling, other reactions to such milieu-induced anxiety may include not eating, becoming aggressive, and excessive grooming.)

In my experience, anxiety is the most frequent cause of both house soiling and territorial spray marking. Frequent triggers that can lead to such underlying anxiety include:

- moving to a new home
- a human member of the family leaving the home because of divorce, death, etc.
- a new animal moving in (see chapter 4 for more details)
- a new baby arriving
- work being done in the home by outside work crews
- new furniture added to the home
- a reduction of time spent with the cat by its owner(s)
- marital disharmony or domestic violence in the home
- roaming cats coming on the cat's property or soiling or spraying on the property
- the occurrence of the bi-annual breeding season

THIRTEEN STEPS: BEHAVIOR THERAPY FOR THE HOUSE SOILING CAT

The following program should be employed for at least eight weeks, although it might take as long as sixteen weeks before

the cat is completely litter box retrained. Remember, *all* of these steps need to be taken to maximize the chances for success. Picking out just one or two that seem easiest greatly reduces the chances for success—or will greatly increase the time it takes for the cat to stop house soiling.

1. The condition of your litter box could be turning off your cat. Increase the frequency with which you clean the litter box(es). Thoroughly scoop the feces from the litter box at least twice a day. Once a week, dump out the litter entirely, clean the litter box with soap and water, and refill with fresh litter. Do not use a lemon-scented dishwashing soap or any other soap that leaves behind a strong fragrance.

2. If you are using a clay-type or a large-granule form of kitty litter, switch to a fine sand–type. Cats seem to like it better. Similarly, if the litter you are using has fragrance additives, switch to a litter that doesn't. The fragrance may be acting as an aversive agent, causing the cat to want to soil outside the box. Gradually phase in the new litter as you phase out the old.

3. If you are using a plastic liner in the litter box, get rid of it. For some reason, many cats don't like it.

4. Consider the location and number of litter box(es). Make sure the box is situated in a place that is easily accessible for the cat so it doesn't have to traverse an obstacle course to find it. Larry's rule: one litter box per cat in the home.

5. Don't allow the cat to be disturbed when it is using the litter box or is in the vicinity of the box. If necessary, place a baby gate in front of the box so any dogs or children in the home can't get to it. Don't ever use the litter box as a location where you can easily grab the cat for the purpose of doing something the cat considers unpleasant, like taking it to the vet or to the groomer or to put it outside. In the case of Ninja, this was one

of the problems; I had to get the owners to stop "trapping" him when he went to the litter box so they could brush him. Certainly don't do anything that may be considered punishment when the cat is near the box. Anything along these lines will make the cat associate the box with an unpleasant experience, and the cat will avoid the box. (Another reason to keep children away from the box is that if they come in contact with the cat's feces they could contact toxoplasmosis, or parasitic worms.)

6. When you are out of the home, confine the cat so it can't get to the off-limit elimination areas. There is *no way* you can get your cat to stop house soiling if you continue to give it access to its favorite accident locations without adequate supervision. Each time the cat urinates or defecates in an off-limits location, it feels relieved, and therefore is self-reinforced for the inappropriate behavior. Taking the steps outlined here but then allowing the cat unsupervised access to those locations is akin to driving your gambling-addicted uncle to Gamblers Anonymous meetings during the week but sending him to Las Vegas on the weekends—you'll just end up enabling the compulsive behavior. This is where structural family therapy comes into play: You must change your behavior to fully correct your cat's house soiling. So, when you leave the home, confine the cat in a laundry room or bathroom with its litter box on one side, on the floor, and its food, water, and snacks on the opposite end, preferably high up. Include catnip, catnip toys, an unwashed clothing object or towel that smells of you, and a tape recording of your voice to keep it company. These will reduce the cat's anxiety about you leaving. Make sure the area is well ventilated and cool. It is my experience that indoor-outdoor cats have more frequent problems with both house soiling

and spray marking than do indoor-only cats. My answer: Keep them in!

7. If there is a new pet in the home, see chapter 4 and follow the guidelines for introducing the animals to each other.

8. Make the areas where the cat has urinated or defecated in the home aversive by applying several different types of aversive agents and texture surfaces at these locations. Most cats do not like to walk on aluminum foil. So, after cleaning up the stain and odor with a product like Outright, let the area dry and then lay some strips of foil on the accident location. You may want to weigh down the foil with something so it isn't easily moved and becomes something the cat starts playing with and giving chase to—triggering the cat's predatory behavior! Cats frequently find citrus-smelling agents (lemon, orange, grapefruit) a turn-off. Spray a citrus-smelling hairspray, deodorant, or other product around the foil.

9. Have the cat engage in behaviors at the accident location that are incompatible with urination and defecation. Cats do not want to eat where they urinate and defecate. Generally, only a cat that is sick or one that has been confined in a cage for a period of time where they are forced to do so—like long incarcerated pet-shop cats— will exhibit this behavior. But the great majority of cats want to keep the place they eat completely separate from the place they eliminate waste. We can use this behavior characteristic to our great advantage in treating a house soiling feline! Clean up the accident location and apply a stain- and odor-removing product. Then twice a day for at least four weeks engage your cat in foraging or snacking behavior right on the spot where it urinated or defecated. Give it some kitty treats, or home-made tuna or salmon balls! Yummie! Very

quickly your cat will now associate this previous accident or elimination area as being a snacking or foraging location and will cease soiling there.

10. Catch the cat in the act of eliminating in the off-limits location and trigger a mild to moderate startle response. As we've said earlier in this book, the only type of correction a cat can make any sense of is to catch it in the act of the crime, startle it mildly without hitting or hurting it, after a two to five minute time out redirect it to a good behavior, and then give it a reward— S-W-R-R: Startle-Wait 5-Redirect-Reward! Remember, you must catch the cat *in the act* of urinating or defecating in an off-limits area if you are going to use this technique. It does no good—in fact it can do great harm—if you use any type of punishment or corrective technique after the fact because the cat will not associate the punishment or correction with the act of house soiling. That's why such traditional techniques like rubbing a pet's nose in the place where it soiled is not only cruel but doesn't do any good. And in any case, you must use the S-W-R-R technique sparingly and judiciously with your cat because with cats—more so than with dogs— punishment usually makes things worse and will have the opposite effect on the cat if the behavior is anxiety- driven. Techniques that are harsh or not administered at the moment the cat misbehaves are likely to create additional behavior problems and do nothing to solve the current problem. That's why confining the cat when you are gone and using the other methods outlined here is often more effective in changing its behavior. However, when you do catch the cat in the act of urinating or defecating in an inappropriate location, here is how to employ S-W-R-R: Clap your hands and say "Off!" or depress an ultrasound device or lightly squirt the offending cat in the rear end with a workout squirt bottle or a 60cc horse syringe filled with water and say "Off!"

(The water technique works best in multiple-pet households because you direct the startle only at the offending animal.) The cat will scamper away. Wait two to five minutes, then take the cat to its litter box so it can do its business there. Then, immediately afterward, reward this good behavior with praise and kitty treats. This is the most important part! Make sure the duration of praise and treat-giving is far in excess of the duration and intensity of the startle technique you used. Remember: If you can't catch the cat in the act of defecating or urinating, don't do this step!

11. In consultation with the cat's veterinarian, consider changing the cat's diet to a more nutritious and anxiety-reducing prepared food or formula. Sometimes if the cat is solely on a fish-based diet, it may not be getting all the protein it needs and may experience increased stress, vitamin E deficiencies, or house soiling problems. Ask your veterinarian about increasing or reformulating your cat's beef and chicken intake.

12. This is the most enjoyable step—for cat and owner! Have some owner-cat anti-anxiety sessions in which the cat receives a lot of stress-reducing verbal and kinesthetic contact with the owner in a quiet and comfortable setting. Since the majority of my house soiling cat cases involve increased anxiety experienced by the cat and a reduction of owner-cat interaction, I have the owners target the underlying anxiety and rebond with their cats. Twice a day go to a quiet room or area of the home and talk in a low voice to the cat. For fifteen to twenty minutes, gently caress the cat and spread out copious amounts of catnip, kitty treats, and the like. Do this religiously for the entire eight to sixteen weeks of the house soiling program and then continue this at least a few times a week afterwards so the cat maintains its level of contentment in the household. It is important that all adults and children over the age of seven in the house-

hold participate in this so that if the cat's anxiety is related to certain individuals, the problem is adequately addressed. It also teaches the family members to respect and care for the cat. This is part of the family systems therapy approach that is so vital to the success of any behavior-modification program.

13. Finally, in consultation with the cat's veterinarian, consider the short-term use of an appropriate medication to further reduce the cat's overall anxiety. Some holistically oriented veterinarians may prescribe homeopathic or Bach Flower remedies such as Valerian root or Rescue Remedy, and that may do the trick. If it doesn't, then synthetic psychotropics may have to be prescribed. Some common ones are the tricylclic antidepressents Elavil or Anafranil (reformulated for pets as Clomicalm), serotonin-focused anti-anxiety agents like BuSpar, and GABA-enhancing agents such as Valium. If the case is particularly chronic, the veterinarian may have to prescribe medication for the entire sixteen weeks of the program to allow the family systems therapy and behavior therapy techniques a chance to take effect. Then at the end of the sixteen-week period, the anti-anxiety agent is gradually weaned away and the cat should be fine.

CAT SPRAYING AND MARKING

It's not true that cats after urinating or defecating always cover up the waste with sand or dirt. Frequently, both wild and domestic cats will urinate and defecate out in the open and leave it there to mark the edge of their range or territory. This range can be as short as a few hundred feet for an outdoor domestic cat or as great as 150 square acres for the exotic big cats.

A spraying cat shoots a stream of urine up on vertical surfaces such as walls, piano legs, coats, and golf clubs, frequently along the perimeter of the home. Favorite targets include the wall areas and molding near windows—especially if there's an invading cat on the premises.

As with anxiety-based house soiling, many times the spraying-marking cat's behavior is triggered by:

- the presence of roaming cats outside on its property
- the addition of new humans or pets in the home
- the addition of new furniture
- a move into a new home—therefore a new territorial range that demands to be marked

To correct the problem, follow the same procedure for house soiling cats outlined above, although if it is clearly territorial spray marking in which the marking occurs on vertical services only, step 8 obviously would be impossible. Pay particular attention to steps 9, 10, 12, and 13.

In addition to these steps, there is another step particular to spray-marking cases. You should assist your cat in defending its territorial range and keeping invaders off the property. Do this by using a natural aversive pheromone product like Feliway, or scarecrow techniques such as shaking a can of pennies or spraying a citrus-smelling agent. Don't leave trash cans uncovered or leave food bowls outside—anything that would attract other animals to your property. Aggressively—but nonviolently—shoo other cats off your property. (Make sure that when your children see you do this they understand that a loud clap and a quick squirt from the garden hose is okay, and that throwing rocks or firecrackers at feline interlopers is not.) This should help keep roaming cats from marking and scratching at the outside doors and windows of your cat's home—those things that trigger your cat's territorial-defense mechanism.

NEUTERING AND SPAYING YOUR CAT

It goes without saying that you should neuter your male cat and spay your female cat. This is best done when they are between six and eight months of age. Unneutered male cats spray mark the most. Although having your cat fixed will most likely reduce or prevent spray marking, "fixed" cats of both sexes are capable and on occasion do spray mark.

Beyond the spray-marking issue there are other reasons to neuter or spay your cat:

- In the United States, 10,000 humans are born every day. Compare this to the more than 50,000 puppies and kittens born in the same twenty-four-hour period. In seven years, one female cat and its descendants can produce 420,000 cats. This makes it clear that there can never be enough homes for all these cats.
- Spaying a female cat will end the constant crying.
- Unaltered male cats tend to run away, get into fights, and roam the neighborhood.

Don't worry that spaying or neutering your cat will make it fat and lazy. That's a myth. Cats, like humans, pretty much are what they eat. A correct diet and exercise (meaning human interaction that gets the cat chasing toys and such!) will keep your tabby trim. Another reason a lot of owners don't have their cats fixed is because they want to breed them—or they keep telling themselves that they are going to get around to it someday. Even if your cat is a purebred, it's best to leave breeding to professional breeders who are concerned about genetics and proper placement of the litters. This is no venue for Amateur Hour. Another old excuse is that the adult pet owners want their children to see the miracle of a live birth. If your child is really ready to be exposed to that, there are plenty of videos out there.

CASE STUDY POSTSCRIPTS

Lisette
Lisette went from defecating in the house every day to doing so only three times in the first two months of the behavior-modification program. Lisette's owners were consistent with the program, and with the combination of confinement, spending more one-on-one time with her, and making her target accident area "aversive," they were able to successfully tackle the problem. By the four-month mark, she had ceased defecating outside the litter box altogether. No medication was required.

Thomas, K.C., and Jeeter
After three months of behavior modification, K. C. and Jeeter were no longer soiling the home. The combination of structural family systems interventions with the owners and behavior modification reinforcement techniques with the cats succeeded. However, Thomas was continuing to sporadically defecate outside the litter box. Because of his advanced age, I redirected the owners to bring him into the veterinarian for a full geriatric exam and blood panel to rule out organic disease, and to discuss medication options to help the behavior-modification plan along.

Ninja
Part of our plan with Ninja and his owner was to prevent the cat from revisiting his favorite marking spot when the owner was at work or sleeping. We also got Ninja to engage in incompatible behavior—eating—at that spot and had the owner cease all corporal punishment. A month following my visit, Ninja's owner reported that the anti-spraying program was going well and spraying had been substantially reduced. As of the two-month mark, no further spraying incidents had been reported. Case closed.

CHAPTER 6

THE JEKYLL-HYDE KITTY

Cat Aggression

A cat pent up becomes a lion. —Italian proverb

A cat refuses to be the object of sentimentality—if she doesn't want to be cuddled, that's it. —Samantha Armstrong

FROM LARRY'S CASE FILES

CASE 1
FILE # 98-00213
CAT'S NAME: Willy
BREED: Tabby
AGE: One year
PROBLEM: Biting and attacking the owner

In 1998, I went to an in-home consultation about a neutered male tabby, Willy, who was stalking and biting his owner. Willy had been adopted from the shelter a week or so before my visit, so we had no history about his early handling or socialization with humans or when he was weaned. However, because Willy was friendly to visitors, and only pounced on and bit his owner, I ruled out lack of socialization or trauma as possible causes. I found Willy to be perfectly social and appropriately active. He used the litter box and had a good health history. If, however, I couldn't help Willy's owner get a handle on the attacks, she would return him to the shelter. As I observed their interaction, I saw that the owner was inadvertently reinforcing hyper-nipping behavior by playing too rough with Willy. In addition, she was continually responding to his demands for attention, and petting or holding him for prolonged periods of time. This was overstimulating him and bringing out the biting behavior. We had to change the entire dynamics of this family system so the owner would not accidentally encourage the very behavior she was complaining about. This involved education on cat body language and rearranging the sequence of greetings and reducing the amount and duration of petting and roughhousing.

CASE 2

FILE #96-60014
CAT'S NAME: Pookie
BREED: Siamese
AGE: Eight months
PROBLEM: Biting, hissing, and growling

In 1996, I went to see a neutered female Siamese, Pookie, who was biting, hissing, and growling at her owner. She had been taken at eight weeks of age from a neighbor's litter of kittens. Pookie was litter box–trained when she arrived in the home. At night, she slept in a kitty basket in the owner's bedroom. Pookie had a clean bill of health and was not taking any medication. She was friendly to visitors (she came right up to me) and played through a sliding screen door with an outside cat the owner had had for six years. When Pookie's person would arrive home, she would find Pookie at the back door, greeting her with lots of meows. Pookie would be affectionate and purr when petted by her owner—until the petting went on too long or when the owner took out a brush to groom her. When that happened, Pookie would hiss, growl, and bite. Ouch!

Because Pookie was friendly toward people and other cats and allowed petting up to a certain point, I concluded the biting was both situation and person-specific: it occurred only with the owner and only in reaction to overpetting or grooming. We had to recondition Pookie, getting her to gradually tolerate more and more petting and brushing, without over-stimulating her.

CASE 3
FILE #95-08314
CAT'S NAME: Teddy
BREED: Tabby
AGE: One and a half years
PROBLEM: Biting the owner

In 1995, I went to see an elderly widow who had a kitty mill–produced orange-and-white tabby she named Teddy. The cat, now eighteen months old, had been purchased from a pet store when it was just six weeks of age—far too young. Now, the owner was experiencing nasty bites whenever she would stand at the bathroom sink or pet the cat for any length of time. Because of the owner's age-related disabilities, Teddy was quicker and more agile than she was and frequently would catch her off-guard with painful ankle bites. Teddy's person was distressed and saddened to see her "baby" literally biting the hand that fed him. If we couldn't work it out, she'd give Teddy away.

Because of Teddy's premature removal from his littermates and mother and, in my opinion, because of the stress of being shipped, crated, and confined in his journey from the mid-western kitty mill to the West Coast pet shop, Teddy exhibited fear whenever he saw another animal and did not know how to interact with people. He would come up to them and was initially friendly, but at some point he would lash out and bite—and stay clamped on until the person screamed.

Accompanying me on this visit was an apprentice animal behaviorist who was experienced with cats. As we sat down and started taking a behavioral and medical history on Teddy, the cat approached us. I let him sniff my hand and briefly petted him and then turned my attention to his owner. Teddy jumped and curled up in my assistant's lap on a nearby sofa. My assistant began to calmly pet him and I could hear Teddy begin to purr. Suddenly, my assistant began frantically motioning to me with one hand. Teddy had bitten her and was not letting go! I whipped out the water-filled 60cc horse syringe I always carry when working with pets and shot a stream of water across the room, hitting the cat in its rear. It immediately released its bite, jumped off the sofa, and scampered away. This was the first time Teddy had ever bitten a stranger or visitor, the owner said.

We definitely had our hands full! Among our instructions to the owner (as well as to Willy's and Pookie's owners) was a cooling-off period. No activities or interaction that would trigger the biting and attacking. Instead, the owner was to redirect the cat's natural play and aggressiveness to appropriate toys and objects. Teddy's owner, partly due to her disabilities, was afraid of Teddy—which the cat sensed—and this only made things harder.

CAT BITES

It's estimated that at least half a million people in the United States each year are bitten by cats. At least 50 percent of cat bites become infected. There are many reasons a cat will bite. Some cats bite out of fear—they are defending themselves. Some bite out of aggression—they are being territorial, either about objects or turf. A cat may be sexually frustrated. Others are redirecting aggression intended for something it can't get to—like an intruding cat outside. Some are inadequately socialized with humans. If a kitten receives insufficient human contact in the first two to three months of life, it will be literally "wild" and practically impossible to handle.

There might be a physical cause. Cats that are sick, injured, or have a thyroid hormone imbalance tend to bite.

However, the majority of cat bites are the result of one of two things: predatory or playful stalking and pouncing by the cat, or rough petting and handling by the owner.

Zoologist Desmond Morris believes that when a cat strikes at its owner because of overpetting, it is essentially stating that it feels severely threatened and needs to protect itself. At first, the cat associates the owner's hand with its mother's tongue, tugging at or smoothing its fur. When it has had enough of the grooming, the cat's mood changes and the hand goes from the role of maternal tongue to the giant paw of a bigger cat. The cat becomes threatened and pounces. In my experience, cat nipping, biting, and attacking are most common in young cats. I also find them more common in unneutered and unspayed cats, cats given outdoor access, cats that reside in an environ-

ment in which there is frequent trespassing by neighborhood cats, cats that were abused, and cats that were not adequately socialized with people during their first six months of life.

A cat often telegraphs its intent to bite through various bodily signs:

- pupils narrowed
- back arched
- ears back or flat against head
- tongue flicking quickly over lips
- tail bristled or lashing

TREATING THE BITING CAT

Before starting a behavior-therapy approach, you must eliminate physical reasons for the aggression. Have the veterinarian do a complete exam—including testing blood, urine, and feces—to make sure the cat does not have a hormone imbalance, disease, or painful injury.

If the cat checks out fine physically, you need to recondition its mental state through systematic desensitization.

1. Remove all triggers for the aggression and implement a cooling-off period. No teasing, roughhousing, excessive handling, or intense petting. Also, be sure you are not overly "enmeshed" with the cat, responding to its every whim and desire to be petted or played with. The cat will come to see itself as dominant, which might make it inclined to attack when it feels you are intruding in its territory.
2. Begin one-on-one anti-stress focus sessions. Take your cat into a room in which it feels comfortable and close the doors. Spread out lots of catnip, treats, and catnip-filled toys. Talk to your cat in a soothing voice as it plays with its toys and munches its treats. You want the cat to

see things other than your hands as its toys or prey objects. Do not attempt to pet it for a week or two. If the attacks have been serious or frequent, wear long pants and gloves during the sessions. Hold the sessions twice a day for twenty minutes.

3. During the rest of the day, redirect your cat's hunting instincts by giving it wand toys, mouse-prey substitutes, Ping-Pong balls, and rolled-up balls of aluminum foil. Get toys that are interesting from your cat's point of view: toys that dangle from a pole or toys on strings that can be wriggled or pulled along.

4. Praise and treat your cat whenever it appears calm and under control. Purring, ears at half mast, tail relaxed, or softly wagging are signs it is relaxed.

5. In week two or three of the one-on-one sessions, begin to touch the cat, stroking it with one finger for a second or two in its least-sensitive area. Then direct it to a ten-minute play session with its toys. Each day, add one additional finger and finger stroke so by the end of five days you are using your entire hand to stroke the cat five times.

6. Over eight to sixteen weeks, gradually increase your petting and handling of the cat to include both hands, all fingers, anyplace on the cat, and for periods of up to five minutes.

7. Pay attention to early warning signs and take a time-out as soon as the cat begins to tense, its ears go back, or it begins to strongly swish its tail back and forth. If you see these behavioral indicators, stop all petting and walk away, leaving the cat with its toys and treats. Return to the session later.

8. If during a session the cat actually attempts to bite you, redirect it immediately to an appropriate toy and praise it when it pursues the object. If it does not immediately pursue the object, startle the cat—with a squirt of water

in the face or a quick blast from an ultrasound device—and say "Off!" Then ignore the cat for the rest of the day. When you return to the sessions the following day, start a few steps back from where you left off and gradually work your way back.

If your cat is particularly ornery and resistant to the program, your veterinarian might need to prescribe medication such as BuSpar, Elavil, Clomicalm, or Valium to give the behavior modification techniques a chance to work. Somewhere between eight and sixteen weeks into the sessions, the cat should stop attacking or biting people and appear generally relaxed. Be careful not to act in such a way as to promote a relapse. In particular, avoid wrestling with your cat or using your hands or feet as toys.

CASE STUDIES POSTSCRIPT

Willy

Within two weeks, Willy's owner reported that the frequency of attacks had dropped from more than one a day to one a week. But Willy had begun to scratch and paw at the furniture, so I outlined an anti-clawing program (see chapter 7). When I last spoke to Willy's veterinarian, he reported the biting had stopped, but the owner, because of her long work hours, had had difficulty implementing the anti-clawing program and elected to have Willy declawed.

Pookie

One month after my initial visit, Pookie's owner reported that Pookie's hissing and biting had stopped, and that he only growled if she ignored his body language and kept petting him too long. At this point, she could do three or four brush strokes with the grooming brush, paired with treats and catnip, before

Pookie would begin to tense. Slow going as it was, she was determined to get Pookie completely brushed in the next two months.

Teddy

At the one-month mark, Teddy's owner reported things were going well. Teddy had stopped his ankle biting but would still bite sporadically while being petted. The veterinarian put Teddy on Valium to help the program along. However, at the two-month point, I spoke to Teddy's vet and she informed me that Teddy had been given away by the owner after he pounced, scratched, and bit her in the face one night while she was asleep.

CHAPTER 7

THE PIRANHA CAT

Cat Destructiveness

You can keep a dog; but it is the cat who keeps people, because cats find humans useful domestic animals.

—George Mikes, *How to Be Decadent*

After scolding one's cat one looks into its face and is seized by the ugly suspicion that it understood every word. And has filed it for reference.

—Charlotte Gray

FROM LARRY'S CASE FILES

CASE 1

FILE #95-41001
CATS' NAMES: Louis, Joey, Lady
BREEDS: Domestic shorthairs, Abyssinian
AGES: One year, one year, five years
PROBLEMS: Scratching and clawing furniture, biting owner's hair

In 1995, I went out on a behavior consultation involving three cats that were giving their owner fits. Louis and Joey were clawing and scratching up the living room furniture and Lady was biting at her owner's hair.

Louis and Joey, a pair of domestic shorthairs, were biological siblings rescued when they were about a week old from a feral mother cat that had given birth near the owner's property. Lady, on the other hand, was purchased from a breeder when she was sixteen weeks old. Louis and Joey were friendly toward other cats, people, and even dogs—the advantage of growing up with a mellow greyhound that also lived in the home. Lady was friendly toward people (she got right up on my lap and then climbed up my arm to my shoulder and begin sniffing my head!) but cautious with other cats. All the cats used their litter boxes from day one and all were healthy.

With Louis and Joey, the goal was to redirect them to appropriate scratching surfaces with lures and baits and reward them with praise and treats for using these scratching posts. At the same time, we had to prevent them from regressing to the furniture when the owner wasn't around. The problem with Lady was that she and her owner had become too enmeshed. We had to more clearly define the family boundaries and reestablish her owner's benevolent dominance. That should keep Lady out of her hair!

CASE 2
FILE #96-00079
CAT'S NAME: Lester
BREED: Domestic shorthair
AGE: One and a half years
PROBLEM: Chewing electrical cords.

In 1996, I went out on a real life-or-death cat case. Lester, a big, lovable shorthair, was chewing lamp cords and rubber doorstoppers whenever the owners left the home. He was in danger of being electrocuted if we couldn't stop this. Lester's owners had adopted him six months before from an animal shelter. At night, Lester slept with his people in their bed, but increasingly his owners were spending less and less time with him. This cooling-off of attention correlated with the onset and increase in his chewing nonfood objects.

It was pretty clear that the emotional boundaries of this family system were too disengaged, or rigid, and not affording Lester enough human contact and nurturing. The inappropriate chewing was the result of kitty separation anxiety. In addition, the owners were doing the old-fashioned and completely in-effectual smack-him-on-the-nose technique to punish Lester when they would come home and find he had chewed up something. This only made his anxiety worse.

The primary task was to make the emotional boundaries in the home more permeable and increase the quality interaction time between Lester and his owners.

WHY CATS CLAW

Cats are not being spiteful or intentionally destructive when they claw the living room sofa or your favorite comfy chair. Cats claw to remove dead nail tissue and to mark their territory and range, which they do by spreading their scent through glands in their paw pads. They also do this by rubbing their heads and faces on furniture, rugs, and their owner's legs. Ter-ritorial marking is seen in wild cats as well. A leopard will back up to a tree, spray the trunk to scent the area, and then stand up and rake the tree with its front claws. The height of the claw marks on the trunk tells interlopers just how big the local cat is: enter at your own risk.

When house cats territorially mark and scratch furniture, they often select objects based on their locations, rather than the material from which they are made. For example, if your indoor cat perceives a threat from a tomcat that roams around the front of the house, your cat might target an object near your front door for clawing and spraying. That's why we rec-ommended that when you attempt to redirect the cat's natural marking behavior to an appropriate replacement object—like a carpet-covered scratching post—that initially you place the post where the off-limit object has been, even if this means rearranging your furniture a bit for a few weeks. This will help the cat make the switch from the couch or chair to the scratching post.

In my experience, cats that are allowed outside access tend to engage in destructive clawing more than cats that always stay indoors. Also, kittens, un-neutered cats, and cats weaned from their mothers too early are all likely to claw more frequently than other cats.

DECLAWING

Probably no other medical procedure used to correct cat behavior provokes as much controversy as the declawing operation, or onyxectomy. The surgery, performed under general anesthesia, involves removing the nail and the portion of bone containing the nail growth plate.

Medically oriented animal behaviorists and veterinarians tend to favor declawing while behaviorally/psychologically oriented behaviorists tend to denounce it. I'm in the latter category. I

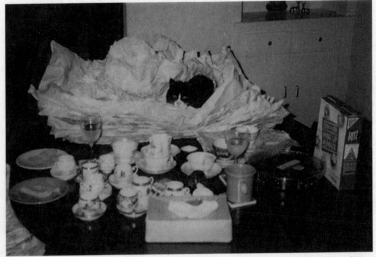

Jim and Pam Carter

see it as cruel, unnecessary, and physically and potentially emotionally damaging to the cat. (For the same reasons, I'm also against debarking and defanging dogs.) In this, I'm in good company with a couple of heavyweights in the cat world: zoologist Desmond Morris and cat therapist Carole C. Wilbourn. Morris says it well: "To remove a cat's claws is far worse than to deprive cat owners of their fingernails. This is because the claws have so many important functions in the life of the cat. A declawed cat is a maimed cat and anyone considering having the operation done to their pet should think again . . . No excuse can justify the operation."

Some of the physical problems a declawed cat may suffer:

- A bad reaction to the anesthesia.
- General postoperative pain and medical problems, which can include excessive bleeding and even gangrene.
- Difficulty grooming itself properly.
- Difficulty climbing because of a reduced ability to grip. Thus, it won't be able to climb trees to escape dogs and, in fact, might hurt itself by trying to climb high objects and falling.
- Effective elimination of its ability to hunt.

There is also the potential for long-term emotional problems such as insecurity, a loss of trust toward its owner, and increased aggression—the cat overcompensating for its physical loss. This emotional trauma can lead to an increase in the likelihood of the cat developing certain physical problems: cystitis, skin disorders, and asthmalike conditions.

TREATING THE FURNITURE-CLAWING CAT

There are more humane ways of stopping feline destruction than declawing and corporal punishment. But before you use the techniques we're about to recommend, give yourself a big advantage by making sure your cat is spayed or neutered. Excessive hormone levels, heat cycles, and turf-fighting impulses can contribute to excessive clawing, destructiveness, and even aggression. These all can be reduced or eliminated by having your cat fixed. Then implement the following program:

1. Get some scratching posts, a kitty condo, and catnip-filled toys. Sprinkle catnip and hide irresistible cat treats like Pounce, cheese, or tuna on and around the kitty condo and the scratching posts.

2. Rub your scent and your cat's scent (if the cat will allow it, gently help it engage in scratching movements on the desired objects) on the condo and posts.

3. Whenever your cat is near the scratching posts or condo, or is using them, lavish attention (eye contact, talking, petting, playing) and praise and treat the cat with Pounce, cheese, or tuna. Tell the cat, "Good kitty," or "Good scratch."

4. Give little or no attention to the cat whenever it is far away from the cat condo or scratching posts. This way, the cat will associate engaging in proper play and clawing behavior with the condo and posts as the main way to get your attention.

5. Whenever you catch the cat scratching or clawing on an inappropriate object, startle it *in the act* and say "Off!" or "No scratch!" There are a variety of ways to startle a cat without hurting it: spray it in the rear with some water from a squirt bottle, a water pistol, or a large syringe; shake a soda can with a bunch of pennies inside; or depress an air horn or ultrasound device. Having one of these devices handily placed in the vicinity of the cat's favorite inappropriate object is very helpful. That's because it is critical you only startle the cat when you catch it in the act of scratching the inappropriate object; that's

the only way it will connect its bad behavior to having something unpleasant happen to it.

6. After you startle the cat and it stops its clawing, ignore it for two to three hours, then redirect it to a scratching post or condo and reward it with treats for clawing the appropriate object. Your cat will soon figure out that it gets rewarded for scratching on its post and condo and is punished for clawing up the furniture.

You may also want to dissuade the cat from clawing by making the off-limit objects aversive in and of themselves. You can do this, where practical, by spraying them with hair spray or cayenne pepper, putting upside-down plastic door runners on them, or sticking double-sided tape on them. However, such techniques *must be paired* with supplying the cat with alluring objects it *is* allowed to claw and directing the cat to them.

SEPARATION ANXIETY–INDUCED CHEWING AND DESTRUCTIVENESS

Remember Lester, the electrocution candidate from our case study? He was engaging in chewing destruction only when the owners left the house. That indicated that instead of being motivated by a territorial issue, his destructiveness was the result of what is known as separation anxiety.

Separation anxiety is a condition in which young children or animals experience undue fear and nervousness when separated from their parents or pack leaders. Many nursery school children and kindergartners will cry, shake, throw a tantrum, or experience a variety of psychosomatic and physical symptoms such as stomachaches or vomiting. When cats experience this type of anxiety, they often attempt to relieve it through chewing, digging, excessive meowing, or self-mutilation.

Separation anxiety in cats is difficult to treat because it takes place only when the owners are gone. Heavy-handed punishment techniques frequently make the problem worse because they raise the cat's overall anxiety rather than lower it. These methods also often fail because the root cause isn't always mental; underlying medical disorders, sometimes involving improperly functioning thyroid or adrenal glands, may contribute to the cat's anxiety.

Most feline separation anxiety cases come from the extreme ends of the age spectrum. It is either a young kitten that cannot tolerate being left alone by its human family and begins to destroy things or cries, or it is an older cat that, after being left home alone for years with no problems, suddenly cannot tolerate it any longer and begins to engage in destructive activities. Lester's case was somewhat unusual because he was neither very young nor very old. However, he did have a "foster child" history of separation and abandonment, which had landed him at the animal shelter.

Each separation anxiety case requires a behavioral program tailored to the frequency, duration, and intensity of the problem, as well as the personality characteristics of cat and owner.

In addition to behavioral treatment, many severe separation anxiety cases require anti-anxiety medication prescribed by a veterinarian. This allows the cat to become sufficiently relaxed in order for the behavior-modification and counter-conditioning techniques to work.

The three anti-anxiety agents most likely to be prescribed are: the neuroleptic Acepromazine, the benzodiazepine Valium (diazepam), the human tricyclic antidepressants Elavil or Anafranil (repackaged for pets as Clomicalm), the serotonin anxiolytic BuSpar, or the anti-hypertensive medication (beta blocker) Inderal. Each of these agents (especially Valium) has potential side effects, and your veterinarian has to first determine that your cat is healthy enough to withstand them—no heart, thyroid, or seizure problems—in addition to taking a blood panel to assess liver function. Also, Elavil and Inderal are human drugs, only experimentally used for cat (and dog) behavior problems. You will have to sign a release acknowledging this.

The type of medication and the dosage will depend on the particular case and the medical history of the animal. Both veterinarian and animal behaviorist should assess the data. Often, the anti-anxiety medicines are temporary and are used to allow the behavioral techniques to take effect. See chapter 11 for more details on these types of medications.

GOALS OF SEPARATION ANXIETY TREATMENT

Can you imagine your separation-anxious kitty one day actually bringing you your car keys and then nudging you toward the door? Well, that might be an impossible goal, but you actually can get your cat to believe that your departures are not necessarily a bad thing—and that they can be quite a good thing. How do we get there? Mainly by using some counter-conditioning techniques, variants of techniques psychologists have been using on humans for decades.

As we first described in *Dogs on the Couch*, we ask owners of pets suffering from separation anxiety to keep their departures low-key in order not to leave their pet in a hyped-up state. Arrivals also are kept low-key—no lavishing of praise or petting upon entrance—to prevent the animal from feeling anticipation anxiety.

Your cat probably begins to become anxious before you even leave the house. Perhaps without you realizing it, it has picked up on certain cues you give as you get ready to depart— putting on your shoes, getting your coat out of the closet, finding your car keys, turning off the lights. We will describe exercises designed to desensitize your cat to these cues and curtail its anxiety.

We also need to make sure your cat is getting sufficient attention through twice daily one-on-one anti-anxiety focus sessions (described in previous chapters), in which the owner and cat interact in a calm, soothing manner, with gentle praise, caressing, catnip, and toys.

The techniques described below are not as easy to employ as whacking a cat with a rolled up newspaper when you find it has torn up a sofa cushion. But they are the ones that will work because they focus on the underlying problem rather than the symptoms. Using heavy-handed punishment to try and correct your cat's behavior—any behavior—will only make the problem worse.

SEPARATION ANXIETY TREATMENT PROGRAM

Here's what to do if you're faced with a separation anxiety-ridden cat that is destroying household items:

- Don't make a big deal of your arrivals and departures. Slip out the door quietly. Reenter the home without great fanfare. In fact, ignore your cat completely for fifteen minutes before you leave and fifteen minutes after you return. Getting the cat all worked up just rewards—and triggers—the anxiety.
- Similarly, don't reward your cat's desire for constant attention by reflexively responding to it when it seeks attention—rubbing up against your leg, for example. Only give your cat attention when it is *not* actively seeking it.
- Reduce the contrast the cat feels between the times you are at home and when you are away. Many people are gone most of the day at work and then come home and lavish attention on their cat. This all-or-nothing treatment can play havoc on a cat's psyche. It's like the child who is a latchkey kid during the week and then gets bombarded with amusement parks, parties, and movies on the weekend. The Monday-Friday world and the weekend world are just too extreme from each other. You can reduce that

kind of contrast for your cat by ignoring it for six or eight hours on a couple of days a week when you *are* home. The cat begins to think; Sometimes I'm ignored when my owner *is* home, so her not being home isn't that big a deal.

• Stage some "departures." Do the things you normally do before you leave your home: brush your hair, tie your shoes, grab your car keys, etc. These cues will trigger anxiety in your separation anxious cat. But rather than leave after you do these things, go over to your cat and engage it in a fun game of ball and give it some treats. The next time, repeat the cues and head toward the door, but turn around and play with the cat again. The next time, actually go out the door, but come right back in and play. Over the course of a few weeks, practice this at least once each day, going out for a varying lengths of time: five minutes, twenty minutes, thirty seconds, an hour, ten minutes. This will teach your cat that your departure cues don't always mean you will be leaving for the entire day.

• Counter-condition your cat to actually look forward to your departures. Fifteen minutes before you leave the home (for whatever duration—even if practicing the staged departures), do the following:

  1. Confine your cat in an area of the house away from the objects it is chewing out of anxiety. For Lester, this meant keeping him away from the lamp cords and two doors in the home that had the rubber stoppers he loved so much.

  2. Provide the cat with a Buster Food Cube filled with its dry food or freeze-dried liver treats, copious amounts of catnip, kitty treats, cheese treats, a piece of clothing that has your scent on it, and a tape recording of your voice. Give these objects to your cat *only* when you are preparing to leave the home—no matter the duration of your absence. Upon returning, remove all of the items until it's time for the

simulated departure drills or antistress focus sessions described earlier, or you are preparing to leave the home again. Do this religiously and pretty soon your cat will be bringing you your car keys and nudging you toward the door!

- Make off-limits chew objects repulsive to your cat. Some of the spray-on or rub-on products found in pet stories designed specifically to do this don't work. Instead, try hair spray, cayenne pepper, chlorine-based products, or citrus smelling agents like grapefruit-scented air freshener. Liberally apply the agent on the cords (first using ones that are not plugged in), doorstoppers, cushions, etc., the cat has chewed before.

CASE STUDIES POSTSCRIPT

Louis, Joey, and Lady

Within six weeks, Louis and Joey's furniture scratching had successfully been redirected to new scratching posts covered with catnip and hidden food treats. Lady continued to jump on her owner's shoulders or sleep near her head, but slowly began to chew less and less on her owner's hair. All three cats were continuing to get along with their companion greyhound.

Lester

Although Lester's chewing of rubber doorstoppers and cords stopped, the owners resented having to change their lifestyle to give him more quality time. They returned him to the animal shelter. This is just another example of the need to get everyone on board in the family system in order to permanently change a cat's behavior.

CHAPTER 8

CAT CALLS

Chronic Meowing and Crying

Way down deep, we're all motivated by the same urges. Cats have the courage to live by them.
                                                    —Jim Davis

A meow massages the heart.
                                                    —Stuart McMillan

FROM LARRY'S CASE FILES

FILE #95-80109
CAT'S NAME: Pine
BREED: Domestic shorthair
AGE: Six years
PROBLEM: Stress-induced compulsive licking and meowing

A few years ago, I got a call from a veteran cat owner who had a problem she'd never before encountered. One of her two cats, Pine, had developed some strange and troubling habits: She was compulsively licking the hair off her legs until her skin was raw. She also was meowing excessively, at times almost nonstop, frequently throughout the night when the owner was trying to sleep. The owner had brought Pine home from a friend's litter of kittens at six weeks of age— too young, in my opinion. Pine had a companion cat in the home, Al, that had been weaned at nine weeks. Both cats used their litter boxes and neither had major health problems— the veterinarian had ruled out mites, mange, flea-allergic dermatitis, and other biological skin disorders. Pine's problem was behavioral.

The licking and meowing had begun when Pine, Al, and their person had moved to a new house. It also was roughly the same time two older sibling cats (yes, it was at one point a four-cat household!) had died. Pine's vet had first prescribed cortisone, which temporarily reduced the licking. When the cortisone was stopped, however, the compulsive licking returned. The chronic nocturnal meowing was unchanged.

A couple of days prior to my visit to the home, Pine's veterinarian had put the cat on the antidepressant Elavil to help with both the licking and meowing. It was my job to outline a behavior-modification plan to complement the medication. It bears repeating: I have found that seldom will a drug cure a behavioral problem unless used in tandem with a behavioral program.

CAT CALLS: WHAT DO THEY MEAN?

Stephen and Valerie Biggs

Anxiety is the key to many cat behavior problems, including excessive meowing. Cats express their needs through vocalization. The pitch, intensity, frequency, rapidity, and volume of the meowing can reflect different emotional states or physical needs. Frequently with both dogs and cats, the more rapid, intense, and loud the speech is, the more panicked, scared, and anxious the animal is.

Conversely, the slower and less intense the vocalizations are, the more confident or potentially assertive the cat or dog is.

It's the same with people, if you think about it. When we are angry or scared, we might scream loudly with great intensity. However, when we are relaxed, we speak slower, lower, and with more of a natural rhythm. We verbally express various needs and emotions: hunger, thirst, fear, shelter, and sex. It's the same with our feline friends.

In family systems therapy, how we qualify or disqualify our words through our voice's tone and volume and by our body language is called *meta-communication*. At my seminars on dog and cat behavior, I often illustrate this point when talking about the "come" command (or come "request," in the case of cats). If you stand tall and yell, *"Come here, you beautiful creature, and get some chow!"* your cat will flee for its life! Conversely, if you squat down and say in a soft, soothing voice, "Go. Scat, you little monster," your kitty may well come up to you purring and rubbing itself against your knee.

Several experts on cat behavior have addressed feline communication and meta-communication. Veterinarian and author Michael Fox notes that up to sixteen different voice patterns have been distinguished in cats. These fall under three main categories:

1. Murmur patterns, indicating a calm, friendly state.
2. Vowel patterns, indicating a need for food, to be let outdoors, or other relatively minor frustration.
3. Strained-intensity sounds—hissing, growling, and screaming—associated with mating or aggression toward or from a human or other animal.

Cats in the wild actually have two vocabularies—one set of sounds for the mother-offspring relationship and another for adult life in the jungle or on the range. Domestic cats, being tame, retain their infant vocalizations right through adulthood.

Zoologist Desmond Morris categorized seven distinctive sounds domestic cats make:

1. "I am angry." What we would call "caterwauling," an aggressive but not sexual sound.
2. "I am frightened." When a cat is cornered, it will frequently emit a "throaty yowling" noise or spit and hiss. Morris believes the reason cats hiss stems from the fact that many mammals have an inborn fear of snakes, which when cornered also spit and hiss. He believes cats are performing a "mimicry display," imitating a snake in an attempt to repel a perceived enemy.
3. "I am in pain." An agonizing scream or screech.
4. "I want attention." The familiar "meow," which stems from the mewing sound kittens use to alert their mothers that they need help.
5. "Come with me." A "chirruping" that mother cats frequently emit when they want their brood to follow or be near.
6. "I am inoffensive." The famous purring sound cats make when in a friendly mood and are submissively enjoying their owner's caress.
7. "I want to sink my teeth in you." A little clicking noise made by cats when they spot a prey animal.

PREMATURE WEANING

I have found that kittens (and puppies) weaned too early from their mothers and littermates have a tendency to be more needy, or "clingy," and often retain infantile behaviors such as chronic meowing, chronic biting/nipping and chronic kneading-for-nursing clawing. In addition, many kittens with this history are stuck in their social development; they don't know how to appropriately play and interact with other cats or how to respond to humans without being fearful or aggressive. For this and other reasons kittens should not be weaned away from their mother and littermates until three to four weeks of age. Starting at four to five weeks, they should have plenty of supervised, positive, gentle contact and handling with human beings—adults and children of both sexes. By doing this, you avoid setting up the kitten for a panoply of anxiety-based behavior problems.

BEHAVIOR MODIFICATION FOR THE CHRONICALLY MEOWING CAT

A cat meowing now and then throughout the day is as normal as you or I talking now and then throughout the day. A cat meowing or crying nonstop for hours, however, is a sign that something is wrong. Here's how to attack the problem:

- First, have the vet examine your cat and perform urine, feces, and blood tests to rule out any injury, disease, or illness. The cat simply may be vocalizing its pain or discomfort. If your cat checks out fine physically, it is time to move on the behavioral front.
- Remove all incidental reinforcement for the meowing. When your cat meows, you must not look at it, pet it, talk to it, feed it, play with it, give it a toy, or let it in or out. Doing any of these things right after it meows will only reinforce the behavior because in the cat's mind it is being rewarded for meowing. You really must have zero tolerance toward *all* vocalizing. By subtly responding even to a low-level vocalization that doesn't sound like a typical "meow," you are unwittingly training the cat to vocalize more than it needs to and thereby reinforcing the meowing on a higher, more intense level.
- Look for chances to reward quiet behavior. Don't fall into the practice of only noticing your cat when it misbehaves. Randomly throughout the day notice when your cat is

quiet. Tell it, "Good quiet," toss it a treat, and keep on walking. The cat will figure out what type of behavior gets rewarded. Chronic meowing will decrease; quiet behavior will increase.

- Give your cat something fun to do just before it usually begins its meowing marathon. Behavior problems in cats (and humans) tend to take place in specific places, in certain situations, and with particular people. (That's why it is less effective, in our opinion, to ship a cat or dog with a specific behavior problem to one of those kitty or doggy boot camps some trainers offer. The problem scenario just can't be replicated accurately enough to bring about a cure as effective or as lasting as correcting the problem where it occurs with the people or other animals involved.) Use this behavioral principle to your advantage by having the cat engage in appropriate alternate behaviors in the locations where it meows the most. For example, if your cat usually begins meowing incessantly when you sit in the living room to watch TV in the evening, before losing yourself in the tube, bring out a Ping-Pong ball or other chase toy and play with the cat for fifteen minutes while you are watching TV, tossing it treats as a reward for not meowing.
- If your cat is meowing at night when you are trying to sleep, take the time to exercise and tire it before you go to bed. Many chronic meowers sleep all day and arise to stalk, hunt, pounce, meow, and explore during the night. This serves big cats well *in the wild,* but all it does for domestic cats is make their humans resentful as they are driven crazy by sleep deprivation. If this sounds like you, try this: Just before bedtime, play with the cat for at least ten minutes and then provide it with lots of toys (Buster Food Cubes, catnip-filled mice, etc.) so it will keep itself busy until it is ready to wind down and sleep. Sometimes this pre-sleep gym class, a form of switch conditioning,

needs to be integrated with overnight confinement in a laundry room or bathroom for two to eight weeks. If you do this, be sure the cat has water and its litter box—at opposite ends of the room. Toss on the floor an unlaundered towel or soft piece of clothing that smells of you. If someone is at home during the day, try to get the cat to burn some of its energy then by playing with it. Any parent with an infant knows how crucial to their sanity it is to properly space naps!

MEDICATION—SECOND-TO-THE-LAST RESORT

In rare cases, especially those more approximating full-blown separation anxiety (covered in the previous chapter), anti-anxiety medication prescribed by a veterinarian may be helpful. This will help the cat get through the eight to sixteen weeks of behavior modification without having anxiety attacks and will give the antichronic meowing techniques a chance to kick in. Consult with both an animal behaviorist and your vet before taking this step.

PUNISHMENT—THE LAST RESORT

All of the steps listed above are preferable to overt punishment. Any type of punishment, especially harsh, heavy-handed punishment, will only make the cat more anxious and the problem worse. However, if nothing else works, try *gently* admonishing the cat *in the act* of meowing. As soon as your cat begins its chronic meowing—when it is in mid-meow—use one of the several nonviolent startle techniques to distract it and interrupt the meowing. These techniques—a squirt of water in the rear from a spray bottle, a vigorous shake of a can full of pennies, a noisemaker, an ultrasound device—should be in sync with a loud "No!" or "Off!," and followed by a time-out period of at least five minutes. Then redirect the cat to a quiet activity and reward it with treats and praise, or simply reward it for being quiet. If you fail to wait at least five minutes, the cat will subconsciously chain together the sequence of events and come to think: When I meow at night, there's a loud, unpleasant noise, but right away I get a yummy treat, so it's okay. What you want the cat to think, of course, is: When I meow at night, there's a loud, unpleasant noise, so I won't meow at night.

Whatever form of startle technique you use, it should never involve hitting or swatting the cat in any way. The startle is only done during the act of the chronic meowing and should be sufficient to stop it, but not be so potent as to make the cat more anxious. If you fail to startle the cat in the act, but only startle it after you get out of bed, walk across the room, grab the can of pennies and shake them—and in the meantime your cat has stopped meowing and runs up to rub your leg—your cat is going to think: When I rub against my owner's leg, there is a loud and unpleasant noise, so I'm going to stay away from my owner. Not what you want.

As with most behavioral programs—with humans as well as animals—these techniques are not going to be like taking a magic pill that will solve things overnight. It may take two weeks to three months before the problem goes away, although you should see some signs of improvement along the way. Also, you may want to consider retaining parts of this program even when the chronic meowing ceases. Not only will that help ward off a relapse, but why *wouldn't* you want to play a little with your kitty every night?

CASE STUDY POSTSCRIPT

Pine

After two and a half months of implementing the behavior modification plan, Pine's incessant meowing ceased and her licking reduced in frequency, intensity, and duration, no longer causing raw and irritated skin.

CHAPTER 9

KIDPROOFING YOUR CAT

Training Your Children to Care for Your Cat

A cat stretches from one end of my childhood to the other.
                                        —Blaga Dimitrova

Ding, dong, bell
Pussy's in the well.
Who put her in?
Little Johnny Green.
Who pulled her out?
Little Tommy Stout.
What a naughty boy was that
To try to drown poor
Pussy cat,
Who never did him any harm,
And killed the mice in
His father's barn.
                    —Nursery rhyme

FROM FRANK'S CASE FILES

CAT'S NAME: Simba
BREED: Domestic shorthair
AGE: Approximately five years
PROBLEM: Acute bowel obstruction

One day in the early 1970s, one of Frank's six brothers and sisters (all of them want to take credit for it) noticed that brother John's cat, Simba, was walking a bit funny. Simba was a plump old guy, with gray and black stripes and a long tail that twitched whenever one of the family's dogs wandered by. On this day, Simba was simply not his normally slothful self. He kept moving around, haltingly, and was rubbing his behind against the piano. The children gathered around. One of them (again, just who is in dispute) spied something that appeared to be stuck on one of Simba's hind legs. The youngster reached for it and discovered it was a piece of kite string. Lifting the string, the youngster followed its path up Simba's leg and underneath his tail until it disappeared . . . inside Simba. Amazed— and grossed out—the Mickadeit kids knew there was only one thing to do. In near unison, they cried, *"Mother!"*

KIDS AND CATS

What parent doesn't feel her heart melt when her youngster comes through the front door cradling a cuddly, purring kitten in hands pulled close to the chest and asks, "Can I keep it?" And what parent in the next instant doesn't see a half-dozen yellow caution lights flashing in her head? *"Welllll,* dear . . ." the mother begins, and often in the next five or ten minutes she decides the fate of the creature—and her own family's structure—having never given it much serious thought before that moment. Many of us have been there—as the kid as well as the parent—and our inclination is often to look for all the reasons to say yes. "It's *soooo* cute." "It will help teach Leann responsibility." And this chestnut: "It would probably go to the pound if we don't." All of which might well be true. And yet none of these are good reasons to adopt a cat if the situation isn't right. In this chapter, we'll try to help you sort through the main issues surrounding bringing a cat into a home with young children.

PSYCHOLOGICAL DEVELOPMENT

To determine whether a child is old enough to physically and emotionally interact with a cat, it helps to understand the development of the average youngster. Psychologist Jean Piaget has broken the progression of a child's cognitive, or thinking, skills into four stages:

- **Birth to two years:** Sensorimotor stage. The child learns to coordinate sensory experiences and motor behaviors. It learns to interact with the world through grasping, crawling, and walking—transitioning from a passive, helpless creature to a purposeful language-using individual.
- **Two to seven years:** Pre-operational stage. This includes a rapid growth in vocabulary, more sophisticated grammar,

and the beginnings of the ability to reason and use abstract thinking strategies.

- **Seven to twelve years:** Concrete operational stage. The child reasons logically about concrete things and can do some abstract thinking.
- **Twelve to eighteen years:** Formal operational stage. Among other things, the adolescent is capable of sophisticated abstract thinking and can test out mental assumptions of hypotheses.

There are social-emotional stages on the road to adulthood as well. The psychoanalytic theorist Erik Erikson believes each child matures psychologically by working through emotional issues. In the first year of life, a child must develop the ability to trust, followed by the ability to learn, and thus be somewhat autonomous by age two. By five they are learning to take initiative and explore the environment. From six through twelve the child must achieve a feeling of competence versus feelings of inferiority. From twelve through eighteen, the adolescent must form his or her own unique psychological identity.

In Larry's experience, it's not until a child is six or seven that he or she is ready to bring home a cat or kitten. This, not coincidentally, is at the far end of Piaget's pre-operational stage, which encompasses the ability to reason, and the front end of Erikson's competence stage, which encompasses the beginnings of internalizing right from wrong.

Among the reasons we say this:

- Children younger than six or seven are still developing their eye-hand coordination and their reflexes. That can make it hard for them to interact with the cat without stumbling, losing their balance, stepping on the cat's tail, spooking it, and generally keeping the cat in a state of sustained hypertension whenever the youngster is around.

A cat subjected to that kind of relationship quickly will learn to flee the room when ever the child enters. This behavior on the child's part isn't desirable, of course, and is reason alone not to get a cat, but at least the behavior is unintentional. But because of the emotional immaturity of kids at that stage, the situation can bring on *intentional* outbursts against the cat if the child feels that it needs to counter the cat's flight and wariness by trying to physically control its movement. Trouble lurks there, both for the child and the cat.

- Similarly, children this young or younger tend to have poor impulse control. When they are angry they act out. What's the weakest, most vulnerable candidate to be a target of their frustration?

- Young children frequently have nightmares involving animals. They can be unreasonably timid or fearful toward a real animal.

- Children, by their very nature, cannot overcome the tendency to be egocentric. The world and everything in it revolves around them. The notion of empathy toward other living creatures is foreign—they simply lack the ability to think abstractly and imagine themselves in the body of a kitten or cat. They may not understand how to treat a pet without hurting it. This human trait usually doesn't change until the child is well into elementary school.

- Some children tend to play too rough with cats because they have a hard time seeing the difference between a stuffed animal toy and a real cat. They may hit or throw things at a cat, and may be tempted to constantly pick up the cat and try to carry it around the way they would a stuffed toy. Many cats don't like to be handled that way by adults, let alone a grabby, shaky child. Not only might it cause the cat acute physical pain, but it might have the long-term effect of creating either a fear-avoidance response or a counter-aggressive response in the cat in its attempt to defend itself.

When a cat is mistreated by a child, it will learn to fear the youngster—and perhaps other youngsters. Along comes a kid who is unlucky enough to try and pick up the cat on the day the cat has finally decided it has had enough. Reacting out of fear and the need to protect itself, the cat scratches or bites. Naturally, the child instantly stops whatever he was doing to the cat. The cat thinks, Ah ha! Aggression works! This reinforces the cat's aggressiveness, since it has just been instantly rewarded (cessation of pain or harassment) by performing a specific behavior (scratching or biting). These situations tend to escalate, with the cat becoming evermore finicky and aggressive around the child, and the child becoming evermore resentful and frightened of the cat. At some point, Mom and Dad have to step in. The easiest solution? Get rid of the cat.

THREE CLASSIC BAD REASONS PARENTS GET A CAT

Cat expert and author Karen Commings does a good job knocking down one of our all-time favorite misguided reasons parents cite for getting a cat for a young child—to teach the child responsibility. The child needs to be responsible and mature enough to help take care of the cat's needs *before* the cat is brought into the home, she points out. "If the child's performance does not live up to the parent's expectations, both the child and the pet may suffer."

An even less-thought-out reason to get a cat: a kitten makes a cute Easter present. Well, it certainly does that. It used to be just ducks and rabbits at Easter, now it seems anything alive goes. It's not that a cat or dog necessarily makes a bad present— it can be a *wonderful* gift in the right situation—it's just that Easter presents are often purchased on a whim, as an impulse buy. As such, not enough time and care is taken to consider the long-term ramifications of having a pet. The cuteness wears off, unforeseen problems arise, and it's Hello, pound.

Here are the top ten reasons people relinquish their pets, according to the Humane Society of the United States:

1. Moving
2. Landlord won't allow pet
3. Too many animals in household
4. Cost of pet maintenance
5. Owner having personal problems
6. Inadequate facilities
7. No homes available for littermates
8. No time for the pet
9. Pet illness(es)
10. Biting

If you are thinking about getting a cat, take a look at that list and honestly evaluate whether any of those could become a problem for you.

And finally, a bad reason for adding a kitten (or, more likely, kittens!) to the home: to show the children "the miracle of birth." In the twenty-first century, when health and biological issues are handled in a straightforward manner in most schools, and videotapes of human and animal births abound, that's hardly a valid reason. We like a suggestion Commings makes: see whether your local animal shelter has a volunteer or educational program for children. "This is far more compassionate than forcing your cat companion to have kittens and increasing her risk of getting other illnesses. Once involved, your children will see more than their share of birth miracles and get a sense of the whole picture."

INTRODUCING CATS AND KIDS

If you have decided your child is mentally and physically mature enough to have a cat in the home, consider whether you want a kitten or a mature cat. The latter will tend to be more relaxed around young children—and less vulnerable. Once you have made that decision, lay down ground rules before the cat comes through the door. Here are ours: never hit, kick or throw objects at the cat; do not pet the cat roughly, especially around the face and head; do not tease the cat; do not bother the cat when it is eating, sleeping, using its litter box, or receiving medication; do not introduce strange dogs to the cat; always wash your hands after touching the cat. You might want to add some care-taking chores such as feeding the cat and cleaning its litter box. As part of your child's "earning" the cat, have him write down these rules, memorize them, and repeat them back to you.

The first time you bring the cat home and introduce it to your child is a critical moment. It will set the stage for the future relationship between the two. Just beforehand, again discuss the respect humans should have for pets and have your child repeat the ground rules. Tell the child exactly what you will be doing with the cat during this first meeting, step by step, so the child can visualize it and will have realistic expectations. Discuss possible reactions the cat might have—that it might seem totally uninterested. Tell your child this is normal, it doesn't mean the cat doesn't like him and if it happens, you'll try again later. Put a handful of cat treats in your pocket and you are ready to begin:

1. Put the cat and child in separate rooms.
2. Have your child sit on the floor.
3. Bring in the cat. If the cat is small enough, place it in your child's lap. Tell your child not to make any sudden movements that might spook the cat.
4. Allow the cat to sniff and investigate the child for a minute or two, until it appears the child and the cat are comfortable with each other.
5. Show your child how to give the cat a treat.

6. Give the child treats to give to the cat.
7. Pet the cat, demonstrating how to stroke it in the direction in which its fur is growing.
8. Have your child gently pet the cat.
9. Conclude the first session after five or ten minutes. Many cats have a limit on how much petting they will tolerate. Until the cat and child become accustomed to each other, it's best to err on the safe side.

Commings makes a point that it's important the child remain seated while interacting with the cat. We agree. Too many times we have observed toddlers picking up the cat and either squeezing it much too strongly or suddenly dropping or tossing the cat onto the ground. This, along with a toddler's high energy level and frenetic movements, can frighten and traumatize a cat and make it avoid or become aggressive toward the child.

A child seven or older can be—and should be—involved in the care of your cat. This includes:

- Assisting with cleaning out the litter box (while wearing gloves and using bags, so as to not contract toxoplasmosis or parasitic worms).
- Playing with the cat after school with wand toys, catnip-filled play objects, and Ping-Pong balls.
- Feeding the cat.

Caring for another creature reinforces compassion and empathy in children.

CATS AND BABIES

If you already have a cat and you are expecting a baby, don't assume your aloof little kitty that never seems to let anything ruffle her will take the arrival of an infant in stride. Your cat will certainly be curious about this new little creature who smells funny and makes unusual high-pitched noises all the time—and that curiosity is itself enough reason to take some precautions. But if you don't handle the situation correctly, you can also make your cat feel unwanted, possibly even make it resent your newborn. Cats are more sensitive than you may think, and caring for and doting on your baby all the time at the cat's expense will not go unnoticed. Of course you *must* care for and dote on your baby and it may, indeed, come at the expense of the time you used to spend with your cat, but there are things you can do to make the transition easier on your cat. These include:

- Weeks *before* you bring the baby home do some of the same things you will be doing once it actually arrives. Get your cat used to the smells of baby powder, diapers, and ointment. Using a doll, simulate feeding, dressing, and rocking a newborn. All the time you are doing this, lavish the cat with treats and catnip-filled toys.
- When your baby comes home, try to disrupt your cat's routine as little as possible. Don't, for example, start banishing the cat outside or in the garage or laundry room whenever you begin to pay attention to your baby. Your cat will begin to associate the presence of the baby with something it doesn't like. That may set up your child to be disliked by your cat.
- Conversely, lavish attention, petting, toys and special food treats on the cat whenever your baby is receiving attention. Your cat will begin to associate the infant with positive experiences. If you do the doll exercise outlined above, your cat will already have this inclination.
- Consciously set aside some time twice a day just for you and your cat. In these sessions, talk to and pet the cat in a soothing manner, again bringing out the cat's favorite toys and treats. These sessions are an attempt to offset any possible increase in the cat's anxiety as a result of the baby being brought into the home. Other than these special

sessions, try to ignore your cat when your baby is being ignored—when it is down for a nap or is temporarily out of the home. The cat will figure out that it will get attention from its people when the baby is around and getting attention too. The cat makes a positive association with the child and wants it to be around as much as possible.

It is possible, however, for a cat and a baby or young child to have too much contact. Let it sniff, but don't let it lick your baby. Infants' skin is sensitive to animal saliva and rashes can develop. Your pediatrician will thank you. For similar reasons, do not allow the child to play with or handle the cat's toys. Do not let the cat handle the child's toys. Don't leave the cat and child alone until the child is at least seven years old.

Follow the guidelines in this section and within four to five months you should be able to assess whether the cat is making sufficient progress in accepting your baby in the home.

KIDS AND CATS: A SPECIAL BOND

With all these warnings we toss out, you might think we are down on kids mixing with cats. Not at all! Actually, we're suckers for heartwarming stories about the bond between children and pets of all kinds. Recently, we were particularly touched while reading the nominations for the American Humane Association's annual "Be Kind to Animals Kid" contest in the United States. In 1998, the winner was eight-year-old Jordan Ross. Out of hundreds of great nominees, he was selected as the national winner because of his "special connection" with the *five dogs, four horses, four cows, three longhorn steers, innumerable rabbits, and a cat* that live on his family's fifteen-acre ranch in Fort Worth, Texas.

The 1999 winner, thirteen-year-old Lindsey Walker of North Branford, Connecticut, started a web site that has information about animals awaiting adoption at twenty-one different shelters in her part of the state. She so far has found homes for 120 dogs, cats, and rabbits, and plans to expand the service to every animal shelter in Connecticut. She spends fifteen to twenty hours a week on the project, answering e-mail, fielding calls, and shooting photos of the animals up for adoption.

We'd like to share a few of the other recent nominees posted on the AHA web site:

- Eight-year-old Aaron Kubaryk of Lajas, Puerto Rico, for creating awareness about the serious stray dog problem in his area.
- Nine-year-old Auna Badke of Bristol, Indiana, for nursing weak animals back to health through a wildlife rehabilitation program.
- Thirteen-year-old Christine Cannel of McHenry, Illinois, for both volunteering at her local animal shelter and leading her school's collection drive for the Friskies Partners for Pets Program.
- Thirteen-year-old Patrice Coughlin of Middletown, New Jersey, for volunteering at the Society for the Prevention of Cruelty to Animals and for helping out in his favorite activity: pet-assisted therapy.
- Thirteen-year-old Patrick Monahan of Moreno Valley, California—the only child selected twice as a national finalist—for hosting a cable television show on animals, organizing fund-raisers for a shelter's spay/neuter program, and using his allowance to buy toys for the animals at the shelter.

If these examples don't tell you that animals and kids can have a positive effect on each other, I don't know what would. (I intentionally included the ages of these finalists to again point out the age at which I believe kids can begin to make the best match with cats: seven years and up.) We hope you take the suggestions in this chapter to heart—and in the way in which they were intended: as a means of increasing the likelihood of an excellent human-cat bond.

POSTSCRIPT

At the sound of her children's screams, Frank's mom came rushing from the backyard into the living room. Being mother to seven children, three dogs, and three cats had prepared her for many types of emergencies. It is safe to say, however, this was a first. There was no money to spare for a visit to the vet. She was on her own. Grabbing the end of the string with one hand, she gently tugged. Simba made a funny little sound and moved forward and started walking toward the hall. Mrs. Mickadeit held on, and the string began spooling out of Simba's behind, much to the amazement of the Mickadeit kids, who were literally rolling on the floor—some laughing hysterically, some groaning with repulsion, some doing both. Two feet. Four feet. Six feet. Eight feet! Simba was halfway down the hall before all the string came out. As the sound of seven wild children echoed off the walls of the home, Mrs. Mickadeit rolled up the string in a ball and, laughing herself, gave Simba a little pat and went back to hanging up laundry—first washing her hands very well, of course.

CHAPTER 10

AILUROPHOBIA

Overcoming the Fear of Cats

There are some who, if a cat accidentally come into the room, though they will neither see it nor are told of it, will presently be in a sweat and ready to die away. —Increase Mather

A cat, I realize, cannot be everyone's cup of fur. —Joseph Epstein

Alexander the Great supposedly "swooned" at the sight of a cat. King Henry III of France was reported to have literally "passed out" at seeing one. They say thirty thousand cats were executed during his reign. And Napoleon Bonaparte would become so frantic at the sight of a cat that he was found screaming, sweating, and thrashing about wildly in his bedroom one evening because a feline was hiding behind a tapestry.

These great leaders quite probably suffered from ailurophobia, the fear of cats. The term *phobia* comes from the Greek word *phobos,* which means "flight" or "terror," and from the deity Phobos who in ancient mythology reportedly could instill fear and terror in one's enemies.

As we described in *Dogs on the Couch* when discussing cynophobia, or the fear of dogs, animal phobias fall under the psychological category of anxiety disorders, which are marked by a persistent anxiety or fear that disrupts a person's everyday functioning—the ability, for example, to go to school or work, or to play outside. About 6 to 8 percent of patients referred to psychologists have phobias, and about 1 percent of these patients have animal phobias.

The American Psychiatric Association lists several anxiety disorders. Among them:

- **Panic disorder:** Made up of panic attacks in which the person experiences fearfulness and terror accompanied by shortness of breath, heart palpitations, chest pain, choking, and a fear of "going crazy."
- **Agoraphobia:** Anxiety about, or the avoidance of, places and situations from which escape might be difficult or embarrassing.
- **Specific phobia:** Overwhelming levels of anxiety are provoked by being exposed to a specific object (like a cat) or situation that leads to the avoidance of that object or situation.
- **Social phobia:** Overwhelming levels of anxiety are provoked by being exposed to social or performance situations involving public scrutiny, also resulting in avoidance behaviors.

- **Obsessive-compulsive disorder:** Characterized by recurrent thoughts that cause anxiety and/or recurring actions or behavioral rituals that neutralize the anxiety.
- **Post-traumatic stress disorder:** A person reexperiences an extremely traumatic event accompanied by fight-flight signs of arousal that lead to the avoidance of things associated with the relived trauma.
- **Acute stress disorder:** Similar to post-traumatic stress disorder but the symptoms only occur right after a traumatic event and rapidly disappear.
- **Generalized anxiety disorder:** Where the person experiences persistent and excessive anxiety without any known cause for at least six months.

The fear of cats is usually called a "specific phobia—animal type." Frequently, a specific phobia like ailurophobia has its beginnings in childhood. Animal phobias most frequently pop up when the child is around four years of age. In children, the anxiety may manifest itself through crying, tantrums, freezing, or clinging.

A diagnosis of "specific phobia—animal type" in a child is not indicated unless the anxiety causes significant impairment in the child's day-to-day living. An example of this would be if the child is afraid to go to school for fear of encountering a strange cat along the way. This was one of the specific fears present with the cat-phobic nurse described later in this chapter.

Researchers cite several factors that could lead to a specific phobia of animals:

- Experiencing a traumatic event, such as being bitten or attacked by an animal.
- Experiencing a panic attack near an animal.
- Observing others undergoing trauma or demonstrating fearfulness around a certain type of animal.
- "Information transmission," in which the person is subject

to media coverage or repeated parental warnings about the dangers of certain animals.

TREATMENT FOR ANIMAL PHOBIAS

Behavior therapy or cognitive-behavioral therapy are the two most common ways therapists treat animal-phobic subjects. In behavior therapy, the therapist attempts to eliminate a person's fear by modifying his or her behavior. With cognitive-behavioral therapy, the therapist attempts to challenge and modify a person's fearful thoughts, or "cognitions."

Within behavior therapy, the most widely used technique is called systematic desensitization. In systematic desensitization, the patient is asked to build a hierarchy of imagined fears relating to the subject of his phobia and assign a point value, from 0 to 100, to each of these fears. For a cat-phobic person, for example, seeing a picture of a cat might rate a 10, being in the same large room with a cat might rate a 50 and having a cat lick one's face might rate a 100.

Then, temporarily setting aside the subject of the phobia, the therapist trains the patient to relax through using such techniques as:

- **Autogenic training.** The person is told to experience warmth and heaviness throughout their bodies through repeated auto-hypnotic suggestions.
- **Progressive relaxation.** The person is taught to alternately tense and relax major muscle groups from head to foot, while sitting comfortably, breathing deeply, and having his eyes closed.
- **Electromyographic biofeedback.** The person is attached to electrodes at major muscle tension areas, such as the forehead, shoulders or arms, and is fed back a tone or light indicating the degree of relaxation and tension. This ena-

bles the patient to learn to bring himself into a relaxed state through manipulating the feedback to create muscle relaxation.

The initial goal is to get the phobic person to remain relaxed when simply imagining the least anxiety-provoking scene in their hierarchy of fears, working bit by bit up the scale of feared situations. Then the patient is gradually exposed to the actual animal they fear.

In a case of cat phobia, the client would be introduced to cats from a distance and over time be brought closer and closer. Ultimately, the client would feel comfortable petting and handling a cat.

With the advent of virtual reality, therapists recently have acquired a new tool for helping their clients bridge the gap between the imagined scenes and the real ones. Watching and hearing the feared situation with the realistic computer video and sound, the client is put in a more lifelike situation than when he was simply trying to imagine it. Once the client can handle this simulation, he can move on to the real thing.

With cognitive-behavioral therapy, the therapist needs to modify the cat phobic's thoughts and fear-inducing "self-statements." Many times, the cat-phobic person is not aware of his "automatic thoughts," thoughts that transpire so quickly—frequently just out of awareness—that the phobic person believes the cat is causing his fear instead of his own thoughts about the cat. The therapist needs to assist the cat phobic person to:

1. Become aware of their fear-producing automatic thoughts by writing down how often they occur and the exact content. ("If I meet a cat, it'll bite me.")
2. The client then jots down which emotion (fear, anger, sadness) he experiences in reaction to this thought and how strong this feeling is on a 1 to 10 scale, with 10 being the most intense.

3. Next, the client cites actual historical evidence from his past to support his automatic thought. ("When I was five, my neighbor's cat bit me and I bled.")

4. Then, the client writes down actual historical evidence from either his own experience or from observations in others that contradicts his automatic thought. ("I saw a cat at the pet store that was friendly and did not attack me." "My friend Sue has a very loving cat.")

5. The client combines the evidence that supports and does not support the phobic-inducing automatic thought ("When I was five my neighbor's cat bit me and I bled *and* I did see a cat at the pet store that was friendly and did not attack me." "My friend Sue has a very loving cat.")

6. The client is asked to again rate his original emotion when holding this new combined thought—a thought that is more realistic, even-handed, and less extreme.

By keeping track of his fear-producing thoughts, rating them and coming up with more balanced thoughts—and undergoing the systematic desensitization therapy described above—a cat-phobic client can gradually overcome anxiety.

Often, cognitive-behavioral therapists such as myself will challenge clients to confront the extreme negative and un-realistic natures of their fear-producing thoughts. As cognitive-behavioral therapy founder Aaron T. Beck writes: "Therapists help patients correct faulty ideas and logic mainly through questions. Eventually patients learn to pose the ther-apist's questions to themselves." Examples of such questions include:

- "What is the evidence for and against this idea?"
- "Where is the logic?"
- "Are you oversimplifying a causal relationship?"
- "Are you thinking in all-or-nothing terms?"

Many times, a cat-phobic person is engaging in distorted ways of thinking to maintain the phobia. Such cognitive distortions include:

- **All-or-nothing/black-and-white thinking:** The cat-phobic person sees things in extreme. ("I will avoid all cats by staying inside my house. I'll die if I go out.")
- **Overgeneralization:** The cat-phobic person takes one event and applies that experience to all other like experiences ("The neighbors' cat bit me, so all cats are mean and dangerous.")
- **Disqualifying the positive:** The cat-phobic person rejects positive experiences by insisting they "don't count." ("That one nice cat must have been very old or sick. Cats are not like that.")
- **Magnification and minimization:** The cat-phobic person exaggerates the importance of negative characteristics while minimizing the positive. ("Leann's cat was nice, but look at all its teeth and how it kills birds and brings them into the house. I know I'll be next.")

The job of the cognitive-behavioral therapist is to point out these distorted ways of thinking and help the cat-phobic person see how they are causing and maintaining the fear.

THE CAT-PHOBIC NURSE

One medical journal tells the story of a twenty-year-old nursing student who had a severe case of cat phobia. The condition apparently originated in her childhood. She repeatedly witnessed her mother go into screaming outbursts whenever she encountered a cat. Now as an adult, whenever the student nurse would encounter a cat, she would scream and experience heart palpitations, a racing pulse, and the urge to flee. She said that one of the triggers was the way the eyes of a cat appeared to her. She experienced the severe phobic reactions even if the cat she encountered was just a picture on television or in a magazine. She was afraid to be alone in her house for fear of an intruding cat, and was afraid to venture outdoors to places she had never been for fear of encountering a cat. More and more, her fear of cats was interfering with her recreational, vocational, and scholastic activities—resulting in ever increasing isolation and constriction of life pursuits.

The student nurse first sought drug treatment, and her general practitioner prescribed an antidepressant. However, after being on the drug for six weeks, her anxiety and phobic reaction remained unchanged. (Drugs alone are never sufficient in providing a cure in such cases, although they may be necessary to help it along.) She sought psychological treatment. Because of her intense fear of being close to live cats, her therapists decided to implement a "graduated exposure" program in conjunction with an inhalation-exhalation relaxation technique. Here's what they did:

Session 1: The patient was shown a slide of a cat while using the breathing-relaxation technique. In this session, she was exposed to the slide twenty times. At first she could tolerate looking at it for only three seconds without experiencing the severe symptoms. By the end of the session, using the relaxation technique, she was able to look at it for eight seconds.

Session 2: A slide of a cat with pronounced eyes was used. She looked at it eleven times and went from being able to tolerate it for two seconds at first to five seconds by the end of the session.

Session 3: Slides of ten different cats were used, then three selected from the ten. As before, she was able to gradually increase the time she could look at the slides.

Session 4: A breakthrough. For the first time, the patient reported having "more confidence" in the presence of cats and said she no longer avoided going down the pet-food aisles in supermarkets. This session also marked the transition from simulated events to actual events. It began by having one of the patient's nursing supervisors bring a kitten into the room. By the end of the session, the patient was able to touch the kitten.

Session 5: More slides and relaxation breathing. The patient now reported that she no longer screamed and ran away when she saw a cat. She was also beginning to venture out of the house.

Session 6: An adult cat was brought in and placed across the room from the patient. Over a forty-five minute period, the distance was gradually narrowed until at by the end of the session the patient was stroking the cat, which was being held by the therapist, who was modeling appropriate nonphobic behavior and adding gentle encouragement.

Session 7: The patient reported that she had petted a cat—held by someone else—during the week and was now walking near alleyways without fear. In this session, the adult cat was brought back in. The patient, although somewhat anxious, was able to hold the cat for twenty minutes and then drink coffee while the cat freely roamed about the room.

Session 8: The patient was left alone in the room with the cat and was observed through a one-way screen. By the end of the session, the patient was able to stroke, play with, and hold the cat, but became significantly distressed if the cat made any type of movement that she hadn't seen in the previous sessions.

Session 9: The patient was brought to an animal shelter where she was exposed to a number of kittens and adult cats. Though she was initially very anxious, her anxiety was progressively reduced to the point that she was able to stroke a large adult cat that she hadn't seen before.

Session 10: The patient returned to the animal shelter and reported that she wasn't as frightened as the first time she visited. She again stroked an adult cat, and learned to accept a cat's new movement and how to redirect an uncomfortable paw contact, as modeled by the therapist. At the end of the session, the patient reported that she was very relaxed.

Session 11: Throughout the session the patient was relaxed and for the first time experienced no anticipatory anxiety about going to the animal shelter. She ended up holding and playing with several adult cats, allowing them to jump on her and run toward her.

POSTSCRIPT

After this final session, the client reported that she was now able to encounter any cat in any situation without anxiety. A follow up report three months later revealed no return of her ailurophobia. The therapy had worked!

With this case of the cat-phobic nurse, we have come full circle, so to speak. The techniques described above in treating a person who is phobic of cats are the same ones I use when treating a cat who is person-phobic.

CHAPTER 11

KITTY PROZAC?

Your Cat's Mental Health and How to Preserve It

She sights a Bird—she chuckles—She flattens—then crawls—She runs without the look of feet—Her eyes increase to balls.
—Emily Dickinson

I soon realized the name Pouncer in no way did justice to her aerial skills. By the end of the first day I had amended her name to Kamikaze.
—Cleveland Amory

FROM LARRY'S CASE FILES

FILE #90-33011
CAT'S NAME: Marty
BREED: Persian
AGE: Three years
PROBLEM: House soiling

In 1990 I went to an in-home consultation involving a male three-year-old Persian cat, Marty, that was urinating throughout his person's house. Marty's previous owner gave up trying to stop the house soiling and had given him away; he had been in his new home six months. Marty's new family had another cat, a twelve-year-old spayed female domestic shorthair named Pumpkin. Marty was under severe stress, with four major changes in his life: a new home, new owners, new diet, and a new sibling cat that did not want anything to do with him—

and demonstrated this by doing the "snake" routine: hissing and spitting. Marty had been neutered and declawed and, other than throwing up hairballs on occasion, was a healthy cat. His veterinarian had previously put him on artificial female hormones to reduce his urination accidents. The drug at first reduced the problem, but when Marty was weaned off the hormones (which can have nasty side effects such as inducing diabetes or creating cancerous tumors), his house soiling returned in full force. I outlined for Marty's people the anti-house soiling program contained in chapter 5 of this book. I also referred them to their veterinarian for a temporary prescription of the anti-anxiety agent BuSpar (Buspirone).

DRUGS AS TREATMENT

The first antidepressant, Iproniazid, was developed in 1952 and was tested on laboratory animals. Not until 1956 was it used in human trials. The first benzodiazepine developed for anxiety, Librium, was also tested on animals before it was available to humans in 1958.

More than four decades later, the medical community is finding itself coming full circle by using these types of drugs to help animals with severe behavior problems. Within the last ten years, various medications, usually among the antidepressant and anti-anxiety categories, have been used to treat a variety of stubborn cat-behavior problems. These include:

- house soiling
- chronic spraying
- vicious fighting with a sibling cat
- vicious attacks on the owner

MEDICATION ALONE WILL NOT DO IT

While on the national media tour for our book on dog be-havior problems, I was asked time and again about the drug Clomicalm, which was approved by the Food and Drug Ad-ministration in January 1999 for the treatment of separation anxiety in dogs. Desperate dog and cat owners were searching for that "magic bullet"; a miraculous elixir that would instan-taneously cure their pet's behavior disorder. The truth is there is no instant cure or magic bullet—not for cats, dogs, or even people.

Medication may at times be necessary, but rarely is it suffi-cient when used alone. I tell my human patients that therapy is a collaborative process; I'm there to help them help them-selves. Frequently, that requires adjustments in the patient's family dynamics, work environment, support systems, self-concept, nutritional habits, drug and alcohol usage, and exercise regime. As I tell both my human patients and the cat owners I see, we could give a person or a cat Prozac or BuSpar, but if the family members still treat the person or animal the same way as they always have, then we're not going to get anywhere. I can refer a depressed female patient to a psychiatrist for an antidepressant, but if her husband continues to beat her, or she keeps telling herself that she's ugly and no good, the medication alone will have no effect. It's the same when using antidepres-sants and anti-anxiety agents for cat behavior disorders.

In addition, medications *always* have a systemic effect; the chemicals impact the entire body. Frequently, this can lead to negative side effects, possible addiction, and relapse after med-ication is discontinued. All medications have five possible pri-mary effects on the body:

1. *Pharmacological effect.* The desired therapeutic result, such as anti-depressants reducing depression.
2. *Side effects.* Often undesirable reactions, such as dry mouth, blurry vision, and constipation.

3. *Idiosyncratic effects.* Adverse reactions to medications that are rare, and are due to a person's unusual genetic make-up. For example, some high blood pressure medication, birth control pills, and drugs for Parkinson's disease can cause depression.
4. *Allergic reactions.* An individual's immune system responds to the medication as if it were an invading virus and produces a defensive response such as skin rash, fever, or difficulty breathing.
5. *Discontinuance syndrome.* An adverse response to suddenly stopping the medication, such as an extreme rebound of the symptoms that were treated.

The possibility of an allergic reaction or a discontinuance reaction needs to be carefully considered by the cat's owner, the veterinarian, and the consulting animal behaviorist before medication is used for a cat behavior disorder.

Also, the animal behaviorist and veterinarian must look at diet, behavior training, environmental triggers, physical health (such as *hyper*thyroidism or symptoms of diabetes, both of which are common among cats), and the owner's behavior toward the cat before concluding that the animal's behavior can be successfully treated with psychotropic medication. In humans, and in many animals, illnesses such as anemia, congestive heart failure, diabetes, *hypo*thyroidism, hepatitis, and lupus can produce symptoms of depression. In addition, physical disorders such as adrenal tumors, cardiac arrhythmia, hypoglycemia, *hyper*thyroidism, and heart valve problems can produce symptoms of anxiety in humans and in some animals. Using psychotropic medication alone while the cat is being treated cruelly or is suffering from a physical disorder or illness will lead to failure.

CHEMICAL MESSENGERS IN THE BRAIN

There are three major parts of brain nerve cells:

1. The dendrite: a receiving "antenna" in the front of the cell.
2. The cell body, or soma; the central processing station.
3. The axon, which can be thought of as the transmitting antenna.

Between the outgoing antenna of one neuron (the axon) and the receiving antenna of another neuron (the dendrite), there exists a gap called the synapse. A chemical messenger, called a neurotransmitter, is needed to help transport a nerve impulse across this gap, or synapse. That's how people and cats are able to think and feel. There are five main chemical messengers, or

neurotransmitters: acetylcholine, dopamine, norepinephrine, serotonin, and gamma amino butyric acid (GABA).

If there are insufficient amounts of these chemical messengers in a cat's brain, then the cat is susceptible to depression, house soiling, and separation anxiety. If there is an overabundance of these neurotransmitters, the cat is susceptible to dominance aggression, stalking behavior, biting as a result of excessive playing or petting, excessive meowing, obsessive-compulsive hair chewing, and hyperkinetic behavior. The role of medications is to correct the chemical imbalance in the cat's brain by causing an increase or decrease in the release of these chemical messengers.

When a person or cat is diagnosed with major depression or a fear disorder, it is thought the human or feline patient has insufficient levels of the neurotransmitters serotonin and norepinephrine. By prescribing antidepressants such as Elavil or Prozac the levels are raised.

On the flip side, when a person or cat is either overrun with anxiety and maniclike behavior, it is thought to be caused by either high levels of the neurotransmitter norepinephrine and/or low levels of the neurotransmitter GABA. By prescribing anti-anxiety agents like the benzodiazepines or buspirone, these levels are corrected and the person or cat becomes less anxious.

Below is a list of the two main categories of medications helpful in cat behavior problems: the antidepressants and the anti-anxiety agents.

ANTIDEPRESSANTS

In treating cat behavior disorders, two categories of antidepressants are used the most: selective serotonin re-uptake inhibitors (SSRIs) and tricyclic antidepressants (TCAs). Here is a condensed list of those most often used to treat cat behavior problems:

SSRIs

Generic Name	Brand Name
fluoxetine	Prozac
sertraline	Zoloft

TCAs

Generic Name	Brand Name
amitriptyline	Elavil
clomipramine	Anafranil ("Clomicalm")
imipramine	Tofranil

ANTI-ANXIETY DRUGS

Anti-anxiety drugs are used to treat anxiety or fear disorders. The drugs most commonly used to treat anxiety disorders are in a category called benzodiazepines. These are used for both sedative purposes (to calm overwhelming anxiety) and hypnotic purposes (to combat insomnia and induce sleep). In treating cat behavior disorders, the most commonly prescribed benzodiazepines are:

Generic Name	Brand Name
diazepam	Valium
lorazepam	Ativan
alprazolam	Xanax

Buspirone, or BuSpar, is a unique anti-anxiety agent that primarily targets serotonin and has a time-delayed action. The side effects are minimal compared to the typical benzodiazepine. If there are side effects, they usually manifest themselves as headaches and nausea.

DRUGS FOR CATS

In working with serious cat-behavior problems, I've found the following medications were most helpful—when used, of course, in conjunction with systems therapy for the family, nonviolent behavior modification for the cat, diet change, and proper levels of play stimulation.

- **Fear-based behavior problems:** Elavil (amitriptyline), Anafranil (clomipramine), and BuSpar (buspirone).
- **Sibling cat fighting or aggression toward owners:** Elavil (amitriptyline) and BuSpar (buspirone).
- **Predatory or dominance aggression and obsessive-compulsive disorders:** Prozac (fluoxetine), or the other SSRIs, or BuSpar (buspirone).

THE "HOLISTIC" APPROACH

As we discussed in the case of "Wolfie" in the cat-aggression chapter, sometimes natural anti-anxiety agents like Valerian root or Rescue Remedy—under the direction of a licensed homeopathic veterinarian—can reduce the anxiety or aggression without the cat owner having to resort to synthetic medications and their possibly more serious side effects. When treating cats for severe behavior disorders, many homeopathic or "holistic" veterinarians will recommend:

- the cat be taken off commercial pet food
- a dosage of B complex be added to the cat's daily regime
- the cat's exposure to possible environmental toxins be reduced

Many homeopathically oriented veterinarians, when treating cat behavior problems, will prescribe such natural remedies as vitamin C, alfalfa, garlic, and the herbs skullcap, valerian, and German chamomile.

Holistic veterinarian Richard H. Pitcairn writes, "It is my impression that many behavior problems have their roots in one or more of the following: poor nutrition and associated toxicity, chronic encephalitis (brain inflammation) following vaccination, inadequate exercise, insufficient psychological stimulation and attention, and the influence of the owner's personality patterns, expectations or conditioning."

DECIDING WHETHER TO USE DRUGS

Remember, drugs alone will not cut it; change in your cat's misbehavior will come about through *all* of the following:

- Changing your emotional boundaries and levels of interaction with the cat through family systems therapy.
- Changing the cat's behavior through counter-conditioning and positive reinforcement.
- Changing the amount of exercise and play time that the owner and the cat have.
- Changing the environmental conditions in which the cat is confined: Making an outside cat an inside cat or temporarily limiting the cat's roaming ability in the home.
- The use of either homeopathic remedies such as Rescue Remedy or Valerian root, or the use of synthetic antidepressants and anti-anxiety medications like those described above.

OTHER CONSIDERATIONS

It's important to note that many if not most of the antidepressants and benzodiazepines listed above cannot be used if the cat has epilepsy, breathing problems, or problems with its adrenal gland, heart, thyroid, liver, or kidneys.

In addition, many of these drugs, particularly the SSRI anti-depressants, can be expensive. Prozac might cost five dollars or more *per day!* And the treatment period will be sixteen to twenty-four weeks.

A cat's person must therefore weigh all these factors and consider the risk-to-benefit ratio of using homeopathic or allopathic medicines. If the risk (major side effects) of using such drugs is greater than the benefit (correcting a relatively minor behavior problem that can be fixed through behavior modification alone), the drugs should not be used. If, however, the benefit of their use (avoiding euthanasia because the behavior problem is severe) outweighs the risks, they should be used.

CASE STUDY POSTSCRIPT

Marty

A week after my initial visit, I called Marty's people to see how things were going. Unfortunately, they had only implemented about 50 percent of the anti-house-soiling program and admitted to not yet being fully consistent. Marty was still sporadically house soiling. I called back again one month later and was pleased to learn that things were going well and they were now implementing the plan fully. Finally, at the two-month point, the owners told me Marty had had no further accidents in the home. The combination of changing the owners' behavior through family systems therapy, modifying Marty's behavior through behavior modification, and using the anti-anxiety agent BuSpar had done the trick.

THE FINAL
FELINE MOMENT

Pet Loss, Grief,
and How to Say Good-bye

O heaven will not ever
Heaven be
Unless my cats are there
To welcome me.
    —epitaph in a pet cemetery

You are my cat and I am your human.   —Hilaire Belloc

When Frank was in his late teens he worked as a land surveyor. His boss, Bob, the chief surveyor, was a big, burly man who even in his fifties was tougher than most of his younger crew, usually out-hiking them as they packed their equipment over the hills and across creeks. One day, Frank walked into the office and found Bob wiping tears from his eyes. "We're not going out today, Frank," he said. "Our family's cat died. We had her a long time and, you know, we're pretty broken up about it." He spent the rest of the morning with his wife and daughter. Frank just didn't get it. A big, tough guy who routinely faced down rattlesnakes shaken up by the death of a cat. Actually in mourning! Over a cat!

WHY A PET'S DEATH CAN BE SO DEVASTATING

As we described in *Dogs on the Couch,* the death of a beloved pet is a uniquely painful situation most of us are not prepared to deal with. To many people, their pets are more than just cats or dogs. They are legitimate members of the family. And just as when a human member of the family dies, the feelings of loss and grief over a pet can be intense.

There are three primary reasons why the death of your cat can be more emotionally disturbing than the death of a relative, especially one you rarely see. Cats, and pets in general, can give us three things most people can't:

1. **Unconditional love:** Whether you have been fired from a job, recently divorced, are dressed sloppily, or are experiencing an outbreak of acne, your pets will still love you the same. Most people are not as forgiving or as unconditional in their love—usually there are strings attached, even if unspoken.

Jim and Pam Carter

2. **Uninterrupted listening:** Your pets listen, they are mostly silent and they do not interrupt. Most people when we talk to them are already thinking what they want to say next. They only hear half of what you are trying to say. This is often epitomized when I do couples counseling in psychotherapy. I'll ask one person to say how he or she feels in an "I" statement of one sentence. Then I'll ask the partner to repeat it back. It's nearly impossible for the partner to do it the first time out because he or she has been too wrapped up in planning a verbal counter-attack to really "hear" what had been said.

3. **Permission to be touched:** Many Americans are touch-phobic. In the United States, "personal space" is frequently a three-foot invisible "force field" that only intimates are allowed to enter—and only in very prescribed situations: greetings, comforting, sex, and so on. Also, many people have grown up in homes in which physical demonstrations of affection were not allowed or permitted. The prospect of hugging, holding hands, and kissing was too touchy-feely. However, our cats allow us to freely touch and be touched through mutual demonstrations of physical affection when they snuggle up in our laps and purr, and when we lovingly stroke them in return.

When these three special characteristics of a cat are taken away from us—like a well-stitched tapestry being ripped apart—it hurts; it hurts deeply. Their deaths can hit us even harder than the death of a human relative. This is not abnormal depression, this is normal grief. As grief counselor William Worden states in his book, *Grief Counseling and Grief Therapy:* "Freud believed that in grief, the world looks poor and empty, while in depression, the person feels poor and empty." In both grief and depression, the person can experience sleep disturbances, appetite disturbances, and intense sadness. But, in grief, there's not the loss of self-esteem found in most clinical depressions.

AVOIDING THE DOUBLE WHAMMY

When a person comes to me for grief counseling over the death of their cat, they are usually plagued by what I call "the double whammy." Not only are they feeling depressed over their deceased kitty—and rightly so—but they feel depressed about being depressed, because the people around them keep telling the person to "Move on" or "Get a life, it was only a cat" or "Don't make a big thing about it." The grieving patient's feelings are severely and rudely invalidated—only compounding the pain from the loss itself.

Loss is loss. Whether you lose your arm, your health, your marriage, your job, your uncle, or your cat—each of these losses are legitimate and require grieving and a mourning period. Swiss psychiatrist Elisabeth Kübler-Ross has famously delineated five stages of grief: denial/isolation, anger, bargaining, depression, acceptance. However, other mental health professionals think that limiting the grieving process and phrases of loss to a mere five is doing the bereaved person an injustice. Psychologists have delineated a dozen or more types of grief reactions people may experience while mourning a loss such as the death of one's beloved pet.

Psychologist Edwin Shneidman writes:

There are those . . . who write about a set of five "stages" of dying, experienced in a specific order. My own experiences have led me to radically different conclusions, so that I reject the notion that human beings, as they die, are somehow marched in lock step through a series of stages of the dying process. On the contrary, in working

with dying persons, I see a wide panoply of human feelings and emotions, of various human needs, and a broad
selection of psychological defenses and maneuvers—a few
of these in some people, dozens in others.

Shneidman goes on to list such reactions to death and loss
as including:

- Stoicism
- Rage
- Guilt
- Terror
- Cringing
- Fear
- Surrender
- Heroism
- Dependency
- Need for control
- Fight for autonomy
- Dignity
- Denial

Psychologist Therese Rando sees grief having three main
phases, which include several substages:

1. **Avoidance,** in which there is initial shock, denial, and
   disbelief.
2. **Confrontation,** which is a highly charged emotional state
   in which one learns over and over that a loved one is
   dead and in which one's grief is the most intense.
3. **Accommodation,** which is characterized by a gradual de-
   cline of acute grief and the beginning of an emotional
   and social reentry into the everyday world.

Worden outlined "four tasks of mourning":

1. To accept the reality of the loss.
2. To work through the pain of grief.
3. To adjust to an environment in which the deceased is missing.
4. To emotionally relocate the deceased and move on with life.

Worden also lists many of the possible normal reactions people may experience when grieving or mourning. These include:

- Sadness
- Anger
- Guilt and self-reproach
- Anxiety
- Loneliness
- Fatigue
- Helplessness
- Shock
- Yearning
- Emancipation
- Relief
- Numbness

Possible physical or bodily reactions to grief can include a hollow feeling in your stomach, tightness in your chest, tightness in your throat, an oversensitivity to noise, breathlessness, weakness in your muscles, a lack of energy, and dry mouth.

Your thought process may also be affected by your grief. You may find yourself in a state of disbelief, confusion, preoccupation, or even experience temporary hallucinations. You may find yourself having trouble getting to sleep, not being hungry, forgetting to do things, withdrawing from friends and family, having disturbing dreams at night, being restless and so on.

In my work with patients going through a painful bereavement, I have found the following phases of loss to be the most accurate in describing what can be expected when going through the grief process.

Crisis, shock. This reflects the initial emotional reaction to learning of the death of your cat. This stage can frequently include panic, denial, and flight. Shock and disbelief are common responses. Shock can include:

- Being in a state of alarm, fighting, fleeing.
- Disbelief. Allowing a gradual processing of the overwhelming information.
- Restlessness. A drive to keep moving to relieve accumulated tension.
- Feelings of unreality. Feeling like one is in a dream.
- Helplessness. Feeling like one doesn't have control over events.

Isolation, awareness of loss. This is characterized by not being able to talk about anxieties and grief because of active involvement in the crisis of the moment: rushing the cat to the veterinarian's office, calling the family, and trying to decide what to do with the deceased animal's remains. Signposts signifying this stage include crying, anger, guilt, shame, and fear.

Anger, conservation, a need to withdraw. Anger is a natural part of the emotional response to significant loss. Each time illness or death forces a cat owner to relinquish more of his dreams, the emotional experience of anger will be repeated. This period is also a time of emotional exhaustion and the need to conserve energy. One of the most common ways the grieving person does this is to withdraw, which allows greater rest time. Rather than clinical depression as many clinicians mistakenly conclude, the bereaved has exhausted himself during the previous two stages and requires rest in order to renew. Grieving is fatiguing.

Reconstruction, healing. When the grieving person is no

longer overwhelmed by fear and anger and has conserved energy as needed, energy may be available for emotional reconstruction

Intermittent depression. This phase is characterized by situational depression.

Renewal. In the final phase the grieved person goes on with his life, establishes new goals, and reaches a level of contentment with his new lifestyle. Often, this person gets a new cat.

GETTING THROUGH IT

As you can see, when experiencing a significant and traumatic loss, many feelings, thoughts, and actions may take place that go way beyond Kubler-Ross's original five stages of grief. To move through these phases of loss, the bereaved person needs to:

- Feel what he is feeling instead of stifling feelings with alcohol or drugs.
- Surround herself with a support person(s) who won't make light of her bereavement over her cat's death. Talk about it.
- Ritualize the loss through talking about the good *and* bad times that the cat's memory evokes. Conduct rite-of-passage rituals such as a graveside memorial service, putting together a remembrance photo album, organizing a family get-together, taping a farewell song, or preparing a remembrance video.
- Allow time to heal. The love for the deceased cat didn't materialize overnight—it was solidly built month after month, and year after year. The same applies to the hurt and grief. Little by little, month by month, and year by year, the hurt lessens and the mourning process runs its course.
- Get sufficient rest and nutrition.

- Take off from work whatever time is needed.
- Consider joining a bereavement or pet loss group.
- Consult the Internet web site of the Association for Pet Loss and Bereavement. This site was created by psychologist Wallace Sife, who became interested in the subject of pet loss and bereavement after his dachshund, "Edel Meister," died of congestive heart failure in 1992. Dr. Sife's web site is located at www.aplb.org.

ANOTHER CAT?

After an individual or family loses a pet, the inevitable question arises: Should I get another cat? This is usually less of a problem in a cat home because most cat homes have multiple cats living in them. Therefore, when one cat dies, there is usually one or two remaining cats in the home. Taking some time to fully mourn the loss is recommended.

I recommend giving it six to twelve months. This allows time for you to come to terms with the death of your cat. A possible pitfall of rushing out to get a new pet is that you will be in a weakened emotional—and sometimes physical—state. Usually the cat that just died was an older animal that long ago gave up spray marking the banister and attacking ankles. A kitten will be hyperactive, might have litter box problems, and engage in redirected hunting and stalking—manifested by attacking the owner's hands or ankles. It will be very needy. If you are in a very needy place yourself, you may not have enough energy to give a kitten. You may end up disliking the new cat and give it away—and end up grieving over a second animal.

It is my experience that within a year or two, most individuals who have been mourning the loss of a pet have sufficiently grieved and healed to the point they have resumed pleasurable social activities, are back to enjoying their work, and can even-handedly recall the good and bad times with their deceased pet.

To conclude, I'd like to share something one of my first pet-loss clients wrote regarding the death of his beloved Great Dane, Thor.

When I am gone, release me, let me go.
I have so many things to do.
You mustn't tie yourself to me with tears.
Be thankful for our beautiful years.

I gave to you my love. You can only guess
How much you gave to me in happiness.
I thank you for the love we each have shown,
But now it's time I traveled on alone . . .

So grieve a while for me, if grieve you must,
Then let your grief be comforted by trust.
It's only for a time that we must part.
So bless the memories within your heart.

I won't be far away, for Life goes on.
So if you need me, call and I will come.
Though you can't see or touch me, I'll be near . . .
And if you listen with your heart, you'll hear
All my love around you soft and clear.

And then, when you must come this way alone,
I'll greet you in my usual way,
And make you feel again, "Welcome Home."

CHAPTER 13

"HOLY CATS, BATMAN!"

Kitty ESP, Afterthoughts,
and Loose Ends

Dogs come when they're called: cats take a message and get back
to you. —Mary Bly

Cats are smarter than dogs. You can't get eight cats to pull a sled
through snow. —Jeff Valdez

A CONTEMPORARY CASE
CAT'S NAME: Boots
BREED: Black and white domestic shorthair
BEHAVIOR: Normal—or paranormal?

On July 7, 1999, KNBC-Channel 4 Los Angeles broadcast a
story about a young male tabby shorthair mix named Boots
that had "miraculously" found his way back to his family and
home after being lost for more than two months following a
devastating series of tornadoes in Oklahoma. Boots's owners
were beside themselves with amazement at seeing little Boots
show up, months after being lost in the storms. Was this normal
"tracking" behavior, with Boots using familiar smells, landmarks, sun position, and magnetic fields? Or was this an example of "kitty ESP"?

A HISTORICAL CASE
CAT'S NAME: Sugar
BREED: Persian
BEHAVIOR: Normal—or paranormal?

Several books recount the amazing tale of Sugar, a cream-colored Persian cat owned by a family in the Northern California town of Anderson. In 1951, the family—husband, wife, and ten-year-old daughter—set out on a cross-country trip to a new home in Oklahoma. As they were packing, Sugar jumped out of the car and could not be coaxed back in. With sadness, the family left Sugar with their neighbors and then began the trip to Oklahoma.

Fourteen months later, while the wife was standing in the barn at the new Oklahoma home, a cat entered from an open window and jumped onto her shoulder. Although it was quite a bit thinner than Sugar, the cat had the same markings and appearance as Sugar and the family joked how a Sugar "look-alike" had come to see them. A few days later, while petting the new cat, the family felt a distinct and unusual bone deformity on the left hip joint. Sugar had had the exact same deformity. The family decided that Sugar had found them, somehow making the incredible trek from California to Oklahoma!

If any doubt remained in their minds it was eliminated a few months later, when the friends they had left Sugar with in California visited them in Oklahoma. Sugar, the visitors revealed, had only stuck around their house in California for two or three weeks, then had taken off, never to return. They hadn't told Sugar's original family this because they had not wanted to upset them.

If this was Sugar, how did he "track down" his owners over more than a thousand miles? Was this normal "homing" behavior, using scent, landmarks, sun positions, and magnetic waves? But Sugar had never been to Oklahoma before. It doesn't make sense. Did Sugar use some kind of psychic-trailing ability?

THE HISTORY OF PSYCHIC RESEARCH AND ANPSI

The word *parapsychology* (literally "beside or above psychology") was coined by the German philosopher-psychologist Max Dessoir (1867–1947). Much of the early research in parapsychology was conducted with spiritualist séance mediums, made famous by such notables of the era as the escape artist Harry Houdini and Sherlock Holmes's creator, Sir Arthur Conan Doyle.

In 1882, the first formal organization to investigate psychic phenomena, the Society for Psychical Research, was created in England. The American version, the American Society for Psychical Research, was established three years later. In the 1920s and 1930s, two men in particular were responsible for parapsychology's evolution in the United States: Dr. William McDougall and Dr. Joseph Banks Rhine. It was while these men were at Duke University in the 1950s that the Duke Parapsychology Laboratory—now called the Rhine Institute—was established and the pioneering research into the paranormal began. Included in this research were studies into unexplained animal behavior.

The theory of extra-sensory perception, or ESP, in animals is called anpsi, which comes from combining the first two letters of "animal" with the Greek term for psychic phenomenon, "psi." There have been various academic studies of this in animals, cats in particular, and they have included the following phenomena:

- Animals acting strangely at a distant location during the exact moment of their owner's death
- Animals acting strangely just prior to an impending disaster

- Animals, including cats, engaging in "psi-trailing." After being deserted by their owners, they travel many miles to rejoin them, covering territory they have never seen before.
- Animals foretelling the owner's *unexpected* return home.

In one experiment at Rhine's lab, researchers, after controlling for odor and visual cues, randomly placed food items under one of two inverted cups, giving the cat being tested a 50-50 chance of guessing correctly as to which cup contained the food item. The cats tested scored "well above the chance level, indicating that 'something' at a higher level of psychic functioning was operating."

Veterinarian and cat communication expert Dr. Michael W. Fox states: "Some feline feats, when no logical explanation can be formulated, push the rational mind to its limits. Where scientific knowledge or technology to explore these phenomena are lacking, the usual reaction is to dismiss 'psychic' phenomena as pure chance or figments of a sensationalist's imagination. The door to further inquiry slams shut and, regrettably, our mechanistic and Cyclopean approach has prevented exploration into the fascinating fringe areas between science and metaphysics . . ."

Sigmund Freud, the founder of psychoanalysis and modern psychology, believed in ESP. He theorized that ESP was an "archaic" method of communication between individuals that was later supplanted by the more efficient method of "sensory communication."

Further, Freud was a member of both the British and American Societies for Psychical Research and in 1924 wrote to his biographer, Ernest Jones, that he was ready to lend the support of psychoanalysis to the matter of "telepathy." But Jones, fearing this would discredit Freud, persuaded him not to do this. He also prevented Freud from reading an essay he had written entitled "Psychoanalysis and Telepathy" at the 1922 meeting of the International Psycho-analytic Congress. The essay was published only after Freud's death.

MANY NOT CONVINCED

Parapsychology and the study of psychic phenomena have had a tough time winning over mainstream academicians. There has been much criticism and skepticism. This is mainly due, in my opinion, to the following:

- Early experiments, like those done at Duke, have not been widely replicated at other laboratories.
- Fraud is rampant in this field, both by so-called experimenters—who fake results to get a name for themselves and to get continued research funding (the old "publish-or-perish" dilemma)—and by human subjects who claim to have psychic or paranormal abilities.
- Regular science—particularly the fields of psychology, neuroscience, psychoneuroimmunology, and biology—is increasingly discovering abilities in humans and animals that were never before thought to exist, explaining away "paranormal" phenomena within the bounds of current scientific understanding. The subject matter or "turf" lending itself to paranormal claims, therefore, has shrunk and continues to get smaller and smaller.

The well-known zoologist Desmond Morris believes that even though many people believe cats have ESP, they in fact do not. Most of the apparent "psychic ability" attributed to cats, according to Morris, can be explained by the cat's finely tuned "normal" senses of hearing, smell, sight, and touch, or through the manipulation of normally occurring magnetic fields, as similarly used for navigation by homing pigeons.

It has been shown, for example, that the homing instincts of cats are inhibited by magnets, lending credibility to the theory that when cats find their owners over long distances, it is not anpsi, or animal ESP, that is being utilized, but the earth's magnetic fields that are being tapped. Similarly, because cats have the ability to hear and smell things outside of humans' range, their "predictions" of disasters can be explained by the imperceptible vibrations and sound frequencies or barometric changes emitted prior to an earthquake, thunderstorm, or tornado.

Morris says: "If we find that magnets attached to cats will upset their ability to find their way home, then we are beginning, very dimly, to understand the amazing homing abilities that the animals have evolved over a long period of time. If we find that cats are sensitive to very small vibrations or changes in the static electricity of their environment, then we might come to understand how they can predict earthquakes . . ."

Morris believes that the many "psi-trailing" stories are merely cases of mistaken identity. There are only so many different varieties of coat color for domestic shorthairs or "moggies" (mixed breeds), Morris says, and frequently the long-lost cat that miraculously shows up may look a lot like the owner's original cat but is not the same one at all.

James "The Amazing" Randi, a magician, mentalist, and escape artist extraordinaire, has been debunking fraudulent psychics, mediums, and faith healers for two decades. Randi, the author of *The Magic of Uri Geller* and *Flim-Flam,* has since the 1970s carried around a personal check for $10,000 to give to anyone who can perform "one paranormal feat of ANY kind under the proper observing conditions." To this day, Randi says, "not one nickel has ever been forfeited."

I met Randi at his home in the summer of 1978 and we discussed the "spoon-bending" feats of "psychic" Uri Geller, the "levitation" ability of magician Doug Henning (who sadly died on February 7, 2000), and the "psychic surgery operations" performed by faith healers in the Philippines. Randi demonstrated for me and my colleague, Stephen Feig, now an osteopathic physician, just how such feats can be faked and readily tore into the all too loose conditions present at most parapsychology laboratories when testing people with claims of paranormal abilities.

Randi's bottom line on paranormal phenomena can be summed up with what he wrote in *Flim-Flam*: "[My research committee] does not deny that such things [psychic phenomena] *may* exist, nor do I, personally. However, in light of my considerable experience in examining such matters, I will say that my assigned probability for the reality of paranormal powers approaches zero *very* closely. I cannot prove that these powers do *not* exist, I can only show that the evidence for them does not hold up under examination . . ."

Randi's organization from the 1970s, the Committee for the Scientific Investigation of Claims of the Paranormal, wants to see such claims subjected to the same standards of proof required for other scientific discoveries. As the then-executive director of the committee told *Time* magazine several years ago, "If we did turn up evidence that a claim was correct, we'd be fools not to get very excited about it."

So do animals have some kind of special sixth sense? For anyone who has witnessed unexplained activity around their pet, it's hard to convince them otherwise. Several years ago, Frank's mother was sick with cancer and was taken to the hospital. She was there many days and was never able to return home. On the day she died, the family's German shepherd began voicing long, mournful howls, something he had never done before. It went on and on, late into the night. Was the dog merely howling because his mistress was out of the home that evening, which was unusual? Perhaps, but Frank's mother had been in the hospital for more than a week and the dog didn't act that way until the day she died. Perhaps the dog had no independent "psychic" knowledge of its mistress's death and was picking up on the generally mournful state of the family. Even if that were the case, it would say quite a bit about an animal's extrasensory ability. Of course, there might be no connection whatsoever between the death and the howling. But the dog lived more than ten years, and it never howled before or after that night.

CATNIP: AFTERTHOUGHTS AND LOOSE ENDS

Some interesting facts, statistics, and trivia about cats and their people from a survey by the American Animal Hospital Association of 1,206 American and Canadian pet owners:

- 48 percent of female respondents rely more on their family pet than a spouse or child for affection.
- 51 percent give their pet a human name such as Molly, Sam, or Max.
- 25 percent blow dry their pet's fur after a bath.
- 64 percent include news about their pet in their holiday cards and 36 percent include a photograph of their pet.
- 31 percent of cat owners expect their pet to come to their rescue when they're in distress. (71 percent of dog owners expect their pet to do the same.)
- 27 percent have taken their pet to a professional photographer.
- 45 percent have set up a special bed for their pet in the house.
- 53 percent vacation or travel with their pet.
- 58 percent bury their pet on their property when it dies.

THE DOCTOR IS IN

And finally, in keeping with our goal to have a bit of fun with this book, I want to conclude by poking some fun at what I do as an animal behaviorist or pet "psychologist." Here is some "correspondence" writer Joe Sharkey created in an article in

The New York Times—a reaction, no doubt, to the rising popularity of veterinarians and pet "shrinks" who use on animals drugs originally meant for human mental illness. Sharkey envisioned a future newspaper column, hosted by "Dr. Petshrink."

Dear Dr. Petshrink:

My once playful, affectionate cat, Miss Whispers, has suddenly stopped responding to me. She won't come to eat when I call her, and refuses to play with her little toys or demonstrate affection. All she does is lie on the couch. Please, would psychotherapy or drugs help?

—Heartbroken in Hackensack

Dear Heartbroken:

Mental-healthwise, cats are tough nuts to crack. Perhaps Miss Whispers is suffering from Oppositional Defiant Disorder, one symptom of which the D.S.M. lists thusly: "Often actively defies

*or refuses to comply with adult's requests or rules." You might
consider counseling, psychotropic medication and involuntary commitment in a secure but cheerful facility.*

Although the idea of a "pet shrink," or "animal behaviorist"
may seem incredible to some ("Are you really putting a pet on
the couch—shrinking it?" a New York television anchor-
woman once asked me during an interview), I believe that it
is no different than a physician or psychologist being consulted
for a people problem.

Many of the medical and psychological therapeutic techniques used for us by our doctors were tested on animals. However, until the last ten or fifteen years these techniques were
never re-applied to our pet animals that developed illnesses or
behavior problems. With the overwhelming number of dogs
and cats being adopted out or brought in by their owners to
be euthanized solely because of behavior problems, it is indeed
("pet shrink" humor and all) high time we use our psychological, behavioral, and pharmaceutical techniques to treat our pets
in need.

APPENDIX A

Cat and Veterinary Organizations to Know

American Academy of Veterinary Pharmacology &
  Therapeutics (AAVPT)
Department of Veterinary Biosciences
University of Illinois
2001 S. Lincoln Avenue
Urbana, Illinois, 61801
Dr. Jean Powers, Secretary-Treasurer
(217) 333-7981

American Animal Hospital Association (AAHA)
P.O. Box 150899
Denver, Colorado, 80215-0899
John W. Albers, DVM, Executive Director
(303) 986-2800
email: aahapr@aol.com
web: http://www.healthypet.com

American Association of Cat Enthusiasts (AACE)
P.O. Box 213
Pinebrook, New Jersey, 07058
Audrey C. Kriston, President
(201) 335-6717
email: info@aaceinc.org
web: http://www.aaceinc.org

American Association of Feline Practitioners (AAFP)
2701 San Pedro, NE, Suite 7
Albuquerque, New Mexico, 87110
Kristi Thomson, Executive Director
(505) 888-2424
email: ktaafp@aol.com
web: http://www.avma.org/aafp/default.htm

American Association of Veterinary Immunologists (AAVI)
USDA
ARS
337 Bustad Hall
Washington State University
Pullman, Washington, 99164-7030
Dr. Will Goff, Secretary-Treasurer
(509) 335-6029
email: wgoff@vetmed.wsu.edu
web: http://hsc.missouri.edu/vetmed/aari/docs/aarihome.html

American Association of Veterinary Laboratory Diagnosticians
    (AAVLD)
University of California—Davis
P.O. Box 1522
Turlock, California, 95381
Dr. Harvey Gosser, Secretary-Treasurer

American Board of Veterinary Practitioners (ABVP)
530 Church Street, #700
Nashville, Tennessee, 37219-2321
Dr. Dee Ann Walker, CAE
(615) 254-7047

American Cat Association (ACA)
8101 Katherina Avenue
Panorama City, California, 91402
Attn: Suzie Page
(818) 781-5656

American Cat Fanciers Association (ACFA)
P.O. Box 203
Point Lookout, Missouri, 65726
Linda Etchison, Executive Director
(417) 334-5430

American College of Veterinary Pathologists (ACVP)
875 King Highway, Suite 200
Woodbury, New Jersey, 08096-3172
Dr. Margaret Miller, Secretary-Treasurer
(609) 848-7784

American College of Veterinary Surgeons (ACVS)
4340 East West Highway, No. 401
Bethesda, Maryland, 20814-4411
Dr. Ann Loew, Executive Director
(301) 718-6504
email: acvs@aol.com
web: http://www.acvs.org

American Holistic Veterinary Medical Association (AHVMA)
2214 Old Emmorton Road
Bel Air, Maryland, 21015
Dr. Carvel G. Tiekert, Executive Director
(410) 569-0795
email: 74253.2560@compuserve.com

American Veterinary Chiropractic Association (AVCA)
623 Main Street
Hillsdale, Illinois, 61257
Dr. Sharon L. Wildughby, Contact
(309) 658-2920

American Veterinary Medical Association (AVMA)
1931 N. Meacham Road, Suite 100
Schaumburg, Illinois, 60173-4366
Dr. Bruce Little, Contact
(847) 925-8070
web: http://www.avma.org

American Veterinary Society for Animal Behavior (AVSAB)
201 Cedarbrook Road
Naperville, Illinois, 60565
Dr. Laurie Martin, Secretary-Treasurer
FAX: (630) 759-0094
Email: martinala@juno.com

Calico Cat Registry International (CCRI)
P.O. Box 944
Morongo Valley, California, 92256
Judith Lindley, President/Founder
(619) 363–6511

Cat Fanciers' Association (CFA)
1805 Atlantic Avenue
P.O. Box 1005
Manasquan, New Jersey, 08736-0805
Thomas H. Dent, Executive Director
(732) 528-9797
web: http://www.cfainc.org/cfa

Cat Fanciers' Federation (CFF)
Box 661
Gratis, Ohio, 45330
Sue Ford, President
(937) 787-9009

Cornell Feline Health Center (CFHC)
c/o Dr. Fred W. Scott
New York State College of Veterinary Medicine
Cornell University
Ithaca, New York, 14853
Dr. James R. Richards, Director
(607) 253-3414
web: http://web.vet.cornell.edu/public/fhc/felinehealth.html

International Veterinary Acupuncture Society (IVAS)
268 W. 3rd Street, Suite 2
P.O. Box 2074
Nederland, Colorado, 80466-2074
Dr. David H. Jaggar, Executive Director
(303) 449-7936
email: ivasjagg@msn.com
web: http://www.healthy.net

Orthopedic Foundation for Animals (OFA)
2300 Nifong Boulevard
Columbia, Missouri, 65201
Dr. G. G. Keller, Project Director
(573) 442-0418
email: ofa@offa.org

The International Cat Association (TICA)
P.O. Box 2684
Harlingen, Texas, 78551
Georgia Morgan, President
(956) 428-8046

Traditional Cat Association (TCA)
c/o Diana Fineran
18509 N.E. 279th Street
Battle Ground, Washington, 98604-9717
Web: http://www.covesoft.com/tca

United Cat Federation (UCF)
c/o Georgian Chambers
5510 Ptolemy Way
Mira Loma, California, 91752
(909) 685-3252

Veterinary Cancer Society (VCS)
2816 Monroe Avenue
Rochester, New York, 14618
Dr. Robert Rosenthal, Correspondence Secretary
(716) 271-5454

APPENDIX B

Cat Bytes:
Web Sites to Know

American Cat Fanciers Associations
http://www.acfacat.com

American Humane Association
http://www.americanhumane.org

American Society for the Prevention of Cruelty to Animals
(ASPCA)
http://www.aspca.org

Bill Hall's Cat Tales Web Site
http://netnow.micron.net/~philco/billhall/billhall.htm

Cats, Cats, and More Cats Web Site
http://www.onlinenews.org/cats.html

The Cat Fanciers' Association (CFA)
http://www.cfainc.org

Cat Fancy Magazine
http://www.catfancy.com/cats/default.asp

Cats FAQ
http://www.cis.ohio-state.edu/hypertext/faq/usenet/cats-faq/top.html

Cats Home Page
http://cats.about.com/index.htm?

Cat Resources on the Web
http://www.lib.udel.edu/services/usered/elunch/catweb.htm

The Delta Society Web Site
http://petsforum.com/deltasociety/sitemap.htm

Diana Guerrero's Ark Animals
http://www.arkanimals.com/DGCom

The Doris Day Animal League (DDAL)
http://www.ddal.org

Humane Society of the United States
http://www.husus.org/

Index of Famous Cats
http://www.evl.uic.edu/caylor/catindex.html

The International Cat Association's Cat Fanciers Web Site
(TICA)
http://www.tica.org/fanciers.htm

Karen Commings Cat Author Web Site
http://www.epix.net/~ kcomming

Katascali Birman Cattery
http://www.vcnet.com/valkat/cattery.html

Larry's Family Animal Web Site
http://www.familyanimal.com

National Geographic Cats: Wild-Mild
http://www.nationalgeographic.com/explorer/cats/index.html

Nature's Extraordinary Cats Web Site
http://www.pbs.org/wnet/nature/excats/

NetVet
http://netvet.wustl.edu/vet.htm

The Pet Channel
http://www.thepetchannel.com

Pets Part of the Family
http://www.petspartofthefamily.com

Purina Cat Training Web Site
http://www.purina.com/cats/training/training.html

Tidy-Cat Cat Litter Web Site
http://www.tidycat.com/facts/trivia.html

The Winn Feline Foundation
http://www.winnfelinehealth.org/cumulative.html

World Cat Federation
http://home.ntw-online.de/wcf/english/ehome.html

APPENDIX C

Glossary of Structural Family Therapy
Terminology and an Outline of
Jungian Analytical Psychology Concepts

In order for the reader to fully understand the application of Structural Family Systems Therapy to the cat behavior problems described in this book, we provide the following family therapy terms and their respective definitions:

- **Boundary:** Emotional barriers that protect and enhance the integrity of individuals (human and feline).
- **Enmeshment:** A blurring of psychological boundaries.
- **Disengagement:** Psychological isolation as a result of overly rigid boundaries.
- **Family Structure:** The functional organization of families that determines how family members interact.
- **First-Order Change:** A superficial change in a system which itself stays invariant.
- **Hierarchical Structure:** Family functioning based upon clear generational boundaries, where the parents maintain control and authority.
- **Reframing:** Relabeling the family's description of behavior to make it more amenable to therapeutic change.
- **Second-Order Change:** A basic change in the structure and functioning of a system.

Concepts of Jungian Analytic Psychology

Jung's Analytic Psychology believes that the human psyche is made up of the following "structures":

1. The Ego Consciousness—that part of us which is consciously aware and immediately knows what is going on, made up of memories, knowledge and so on.

2. The Personal Unconscious—is analogous to Freud's view of the unconscious, it being made up of things out of one's past, but which has been forgotten or "repressed," to defend the conscious ego from unacceptable or threatening impulses or anxieties.

3. The Collective Unconscious—which, according to Jung, represents the larger aspect of the individual psyche, which is inherited, made up of images, ideas, and possibilities that are common to all men collectively; kind of like the "archaic remnants" of the human race. The images that are contained in the "humanity-shared" Collective Unconscious are referred to as "Archetypes," the shared prototypes of emotional reaction. The theory has it that over the course of human history, certain day-to-day events *had* to be experienced by all members of the "human family," as in the daily rising and setting of the sun. Archetypes are the cumulative effect of these "perpetually repeated experiences" on the human nervous system's development. It is the **subjective emotional reaction** to these universally recurring events that is contained in the Collective Unconscious.

The Anima and the Animus

One example of an archetype that Jung theorized to exist was that of the "anima" and the "animus." These are the Latin names for the "female soul-image (*anima*)," and for the "male soul-image (*animus*)." Jung believed that both men and women have within their psyches or personalities a part of the other sex archetype: the man had his feminine side, often leading to "irrational emotions," according to Jung, and the woman had her masculine side, often leading to "rigid thoughts" and opinions. The relative balance of the masculine-feminine nature in each of us helps us adapt to social gender roles: women are taught to act "lady-like," and men more "manly-like."

Emma Jung, the wife of Carl Jung, and an analytical psychologist in her own right, wrote in her book, *Animus and Anima,* that the anima and animus are two archetypal figures of great importance and that in a man, these feminine characteristics, and in a woman, these masculine characteristics, are always present.

APPENDIX D

*Statistics on Cat Ownership
and Cat Breeds*

Cat Breeds and Breed Classification

There are approximately forty different species of cats existing today. The domestic cat is just one of them. Depending on which cat breed association you go by, there exists between eighty and one hundred recognized pedigree cat breeds. Recognized cat breed classes include:

- Persians (longhair)
- Other longhairs (non-Persian longhair cats)
- British shorthairs
- American (or domestic) shorthairs
- Oriental or Oriental shorthairs (Siamese breeds without the Siamese coat)
- Burmese
- Siamese

Between 1992 and 1996, the top five cat breeds registered with the Cat Fancier's Association in the United States were:

1. The Persian (in 1996, numbering 42,578 registrations)
2. The Maine Coon (in 1996, numbering 4,747 registrations)
3. The Siamese (in 1996, numbering 2,865 registrations)

4. The Abyssinian (in 1996, numbering 2,383 registrations)
5. The Exotic (in 1996, numbering 1,981 registrations)

In the sixth to eleventh ranks, although their ordered positions changed over that four-year period, were the Oriental, Scottish Fold, American Shorthair, Birman, Ocicat, and Burmese.

Veterinarians more often mention the Siamese cat than almost any other purebred cat when discussing breeds that are prone to separation anxiety (which make sense because of their very, excuse me, "doglike," outgoing and social personalities). Whereas the Persian cat is the one most mentioned as having an increased likelihood of elimination or house soiling problems.

This last point, on various behavior problems being associated with different breeds, is reflected in my own behavioral practice. Partly due to their popularity and greater overall numbers in the cat population in total, I do see Persian cats and American (or domestic) shorthairs more often than any other breed, for cat elimination or house soiling behavior problems. For fighting with other cats or spray marking in the home, I see Siamese cats and, either American shorthair or longhair cats, more than any other cat breed. As far as difficulties accepting a "new" member of the household, or chronic meowing or destruction, I see a good cross-section of most of the top ten cat breeds exhibiting these behavior problems (as will be seen with the cited case histories given in this book, starting in chapter 3). These include: Himalayans, Ragdolls, Abyssinians, and Exotics.

The Personality and Demographics of the People Who Own and Cherish Cats

According to the American Veterinary Medical Association, as of 1996, there were 98.9 million households that owned a companion animal (cat, dog, bird, horse, etc.). *That's over half,*

58.9 percent of all U.S. households. As we mentioned in the introduction to this book, *cats have surpassed dogs in their total numbers* (59.1 million cats versus 52.9 million dogs, in 1996) among the pet population even though more households own dogs rather than cats. This is attributed to the fact that cat owners frequently own more than one cat. The state with the highest rate of cat ownership in 1996 was Idaho.

Over half of the cat-owning households surveyed in 1996, *52 percent, owned more than one cat.* As mentioned above, the Persian cat breed remains the *most popular of the registered cat breeds* in the United States.

The 1996 survey also showed that the "average" cat owner was in the "middle parents" category; heads of households less than forty-five years of age who had children less than six years of age. This was the group that *had the highest rate of cat ownership.* On the flip side, "older singles," defined as a households containing only one member, older than sixty-five years of age, was the "life-stage group" *least* likely to own a cat.

From 1991 to 1996, the "rate" of cat ownership decreased for all groups *except* for *young singles and young parents.* So, the profile we get on the typical cat owner, at least demographically, is either of a single person in a single person household under thirty-five years of age, or middle parents, in a multiple member household, with the head of the house being forty-five or less, and the youngest child being under six years of age.

APPENDIX E

Inspiring News Article/Web Site
Excerpts on Cats and Their People

There is a story about a female Tabby named "Bart," who lives in Illinois with a high school student named Jose. A few years ago, during the night, while Bart and Jose slept, Jose began convulsing from a life-threatening seizure. Bart, apparently alarmed by Jose's distress, ran out of the room, down the hallway, and leapt upon the mother's bed in the next room. As Jose later related to *WNET-TV* in New York, "She was licking my mom's eyelids, scratching and meowing, doing anything she could to wake her up." The warning worked: Jose made it to a nearby hospital and his life was saved. And, in a historic first, the Illinois state government honored Bart for her "ingenuity and persistence" in the rescue. Bart was indeed the "hero" cat from Illinois!

Bill Hall, a columnist for the *Lewiston Tribune,* writes that he recently received a "disconcerting compliment" from a woman veterinarian that caused him to reassure his readers about his "manhood." After Hall told the veterinarian that he loved and admired cats, the veterinarian told him, "We still see some men who are embarrassed to admit they care about a cat." Hall took that comment to imply that there may be some kind of a general stereotype in our society that says it is "unmanly" to own a cat. As he writes: "While it is true that I hang out with cats, you have to understand that these are very tough cats we're talking about here. These are pretty rough customers—big, brawny brute cats who snarl at strangers and bring huge, dangerous mice home day after day . . ."

Hall goes on to challenge the myth that only "manly" men own dogs, and less-than-manly men own cats. He points out that: "Some of us are so brave, so manly that we dare go forth each day (in boots and married to our woman) protected only by a very small animal. But don't get any ideas. If you should be foolish enough to try anything, be warned that I have at my side a killer cat . . . eight pounds of death ready to strike. Be warned as well that a cat also has hair on its chest."

APPENDIX F

The Diary of a Cat Owner—A Comprehensive Treatment Review of the Case of "Wolfie and the Trespassing Tom," by Wolfie's Mom: From Beginning to End

Wolfie's Story

On October 25, 1998, a stray cat was on the porch patio right outside of the bedroom window where my indoor cats watch the birds all day. I purposely put several plants and bird feeders on the porch for entertainment value for my cats, and because it was very peaceful. As it turns out, the other cats in the neighborhood thought it was nice, too. On the 25th, I found a stray cat on my porch twice that day; two different cats at two different times.

Unbeknownst to me, the outdoor cats must have really upset Wolfie, as his behavior changed radically. All four of my cats are from the same litter, have grown up together, and have never been apart from each other. All of a sudden (after the stray cat sighting), Wolfie and Java (the two males) were seriously at odds with each other. Wolfie was making a low, deep growling sound later that evening and was very unsettled. Little did I know how upset he was, and it took me a while to figure out what had occurred. At 1:30 A.M. that night, I woke up to Wolfie hissing, growling, and fighting with Java. When I got out of bed, the fight broke up. I gave both males the fear and stress homeopathic formula. At 3:30 A.M. Wolfie and Java started fighting again. I then started giving them Valerian and water in a dropper, to no avail. I finally gave both males a dropper of straight Valerian; this seemed to help somewhat, but not enough.

For the next twenty-four hours, I continued to give Wolfie the Acepromozine and also gave ½ a tablet to Java. I put Wolfie into the bathroom for a while. When I went back there, I found Wolfie crouched in his kitty pan (not to use it, though). He was looking pretty woozy by then. He insists on hiding in or behind something—very fearful. The Acepromozine affects Wolfie much more than it does Java; even though Wolfie weighs about one or two pounds more.

That next morning, I noticed that Wolfie smelled like a wild goat so I gave him a bath. I also had to wash the other three so that they would all smell the same. I spoke with Dr. Gordon and he recommended that I use a spray called Feliway, a pheromone spray. Unfortunately, this did not work. Dr. Gordon advised me that we could end up on drug therapy and then gave me your telephone number. At the same time, Dr. Gordon approved of giving Wolfie 10 mg. of Acepromozine. This definitely calmed Wolfie down. On October 26th, I left a message for you.

10/26–11/6   Wolfie continues to be separated from the other three. He is very fearful. Wolfie is requiring more attention from me than he has in the past. Previously, Wolfie was always very aloof. He was also the lead cat. He now comes up to sit on my lap and purrs, I think more out of fear than anything. I give him as much attention as possible. The other three will hiss at the door when they know Wolfie is near. We play at the door, under it, with toys, and this seems to lessen the hissing somewhat. Not much interaction under the door, though. They have all been getting Valerian their food, but Wolfie gets more. Only helps a little. During this time, Wolfie has started spraying the kitty pan routinely. He did do this before, but only a few times a week. Now it is daily.

11/8/98   Met with Larry Lachman and went over the history of all four and discussed what happened to cause this problem. Larry outlined a program that will last approximately twelve weeks and will also include a RX for Wolfie, which is Buspar and Acepromozine for the other three as needed.

11/9/98   Picked up BuSpar (10 mg.) for Wolfie and started at ½ a tablet per day, ¼ of a 10 mg. tablet of Acepromozine for the others. I also picked up liverwurst, string cheese, and Brie cheese. Put the pills in the liverwurst for India and Java. Had to use turkey for Wolfie and Blanca. Started the kitty exercises tonight approximately one hour after giving them the Acepromozine. Put Wolfie on a leash and harness at one end of the living room. His leash is secured to a dining room chair. Brought each cat out individually in a leash and harness. All were more concerned about the leash and harness than Wolfie. Each was out about fifteen minutes. Wolfie was pretty far away, but they could see him. Wolfie started to hide toward the end of the exercises. Too much exposure, I guess, for the first time.

Continued status quo from 11/9/98–11/28/98; took turns bringing one cat out at a time. Still very far away from Wolfie but they can see him.   11/29/99 Increased BuSpar to 1½ tablets per day after discussing the situation with Dr. Gordon. Wolfie is still spraying the kitty pan. Java is doing okay with the reconditioning exercises, however, his tail is pretty active (smacking). I can get him to play with the feather toy while he is out with Wolfie. I use treats of course. India is also doing well. She will play and is definitely swayed by treats. Blanca was doing well until I scared her with the metallic spangle toy. Now I have to work on getting her to be comfortable again. I keep her in my lap and I eventually get her to eat treats. Her fear is not of Wolfie but of the toy. The harnesses affect all of the cats behaviorally. Java is the least concerned but all undergo a transformation while wearing a harness. Wolfie seems really ready to join the others. He seems very lonely but is doing well with the rotation and stuff.

12/2/98   Wolfie still sprays the kitty pan. Other than this he seems fine. Spends a lot of time sitting outside the bedroom door where the others are contained inside. India is progressing the best of the three with the reconditioning exercises. Again, her primary interest is in the treats; she's a bit of a pig. She knows Wolfie is in the room, but does not pay much attention to him. Java is still irritated with Wolfie being in the room. Java got very close to Wolfie last night, about one foot away. No hissing, but he did let out little cries. He did this several times. I just kept moving Java away. Wolfie is not as comfortable with Java as he is with the girls. I pay very close attention to the body language of each cat. They are actually very easy to read. Blanca is very interested in Wolfie's bathroom (when he is contained, it's in the bathroom). While he is secured by leash and harness, she will go into the bathroom and smell around and will even lay in Wolfie's carrier. All three cats are now within two feet of Wolfie when we are doing our exercises. I need to ignore Java more in order to encourage him to have better behavior while Wolfie is out with him.

12/5/98   Wolfie is now on one tablet of BuSpar each morning and evening. The other three are still on Acepromozine as they are still uptight while Wolfie is out during exercise time.

Observation. India and Java will turn their backs on Wolfie while they are out exercising, seems like they are ignoring him in this manner but they still know that he is there. Java is still on Acepromozine. I know that I can't trust him yet. Blanca pulls out of her leash and harness by backing up out of it. She seems okay off the leash and I keep a very close eye on her when she wiggles out. Wolfie seems okay, but is keenly aware of Blanca walking around. Wolfie is not responding well to being on the leash and harness. He gets very agitated, but doesn't have a choice. We have been working on the integration for about six weeks now. This is about the halfway mark. I can see why this takes so long. Can't trust cats, and you need lots of patience.

12/19/98   This morning I hooked Wolfie up to the dining room chair (leash and harness secured to the chair at the far end of the living room). While I was in the bedroom getting the others into their harnesses, I heard a very loud crash. When I came out to see what had happened, I found the chair knocked over and Wolfie was tangled up in his leash. I had a hard time extracting him. He was totally freaked out and was trembling, so I put him in the bathroom with a few chunks of liverwurst. He stayed very quiet for about two hours. We were not able to do our exercises because of this. I can see that patience is the key here.

12/30/98   On 12/28 I was finally able to get Wolfie calm enough to be able to put his harness and leash on him and bring out another cat. This has taken a good deal of time to get back to this point in the routine. To get here, I just kept Wolfie in his harness for long periods of time (while he was in the bathroom and/or while he was around the house and the others were confined to the bedroom). On 12/29/98 I brought Wolfie out and then India. A little later during the exercise time, I brought Java out while India was still out. This went well. No hissing, growling, or crying from anyone. This progress is encouraging.

1/3/99   Discussed BuSpar RX with Dr. Gordon, started reducing the dosage of BuSpar for Wolfie. He now receives one tablet in the AM and only ½ a tablet in the PM. 1/4/99   Decreased dose of BuSpar again to ½ a tablet in the AM and PM. 1/5/99   Just ½ a tablet of BuSpar in the

AM, none in the PM. 1/6/99 Started Elavil, 10 mg. ½ a tablet in the AM and ½ in the PM. Wolfie will not eat his food at all. He is lethargic and agitated, has some serious tail smacking going on. Gave Wolfie ⅓ of a tablet in liverwurst until he got wise to me. Unusual behavior, a little more fearful and agitated. Stools are smelly and runny. Three stools today. Wolfie does not seem to be himself. No exercise tonight or yesterday. 1/12/99 Gave Wolfie ½ a tablet of Elavil in the AM. Did not give him any more after that. Wolfie won't eat, only nibbles. He is no longer friendly. Some how this is the wrong RX for him. I am discontinuing the med. Will talk to Dr. Gordon.

1/16/99   Wolfie is back to normal. No more meds. He eats and talks to me and rubs against me. Much more himself. Hates being on harness and leash but will tolerate it. Likes roast pork. I used this as a small treat tonight. I no longer focus on treats, but I do use them still. I use the fishing pole toy, too. This evening I had Wolfie out, and then brought Java and India out, too. Both were very happy for their treats (pigs in cats' clothing). They are all in harnesses and leashes. Java tried to get very close to Wolfie a few times, so I finally let him, as I had my horse squirter. Java was reaching out to Wolfie, who was lying down. Java was trying to touch Wolfie with his paw, and did so. Wolfie stayed clam. Java then inched right up to Wolfie's nose and they both smelled each other's mouths. No problems! No hissing, growling, or crying. Later on, Java went and lay down fairly close to Wolfie, maybe twelve inches away. Both cats had positive body language. Java loves to play with the fishing pole toy. Wolfie plays a little. Wolfie will play when others are out but not as much as when he is by himself. Blanca was allowed to roam free. She chose to stay in the bedroom. All in all, I am very happy with how things are going.

————

1/27/99   Wolfie has become very social recently. Wants to be with me. Cries if he is by himself and I am in the house. Really likes to be petted now. This is very different behavior than what I am accustomed to. Wolfie has always been very standoffish, probably not socialized as much as he needed to be. I see this with all of them except Java. Guess this comes from being born wild and taken away from their momma cat when they were ten days old. They then spent the next five weeks in a rabbit hutch with a semi-feral substitute momma cat who had just finished nursing her own litter.

2/19/99   I have been trying for the last two weeks to get Wolfie comfortable again, especially with Java. I was bringing all three out with Wolfie and no one was comfortable. This just wasn't working. About two or three weeks ago, Wolfie scared Java when Java came around the living room chair and ran into Wolfie. There was hissing from Java and even crying once. This was a major setback. Because of this, I then decided to bring Java out by himself. I was able to get the best results with Wolfie by using sliced turkey, as he *loves* it. Doing one-on-one has been working. I give Java lots of love and attention. Things have been going well with the two. Java plays a lot— very happy. Wolfie is more reserved and only plays a little, but he does seem to be okay. Tonight I started out with Wolfie and Java and since they were doing so well, I brought out Blanca and India. It was an excellent exercise. All were comfortable. Wolfie didn't try to hide. I kept them out for approximately one hour. Yippee!

3/4/99   All doing very well with exercise. I give them the thickly sliced honey-cured turkey from the deli, cut into squares. Wolfie puts aside any fears in order to get his turkey. We have treats, and then we play with the stick end of the pole toy. I run the stick end of the toy under the little entryway carpet. They all like this. They pounce and bat at the carpet. They get very close to Wolfie and vice versa. Java and Wolfie have come nose to nose without any hissing or growling. Last night when Wolfie got too close (very close) to India she hissed and was promptly put away in the bedroom. Blanca did the same two nights ago but this is uncommon for both girls. Wolfie is getting much more comfortable and, therefore, closer to the others. This evening Java jumped while playing and really scared all of the other cats. They all recovered well, no paranoia. Our time out is about one hour. Wolfie is much more relaxed. We will stick with this routine for a while longer. We have been doing it for about two weeks. Wolfie is still very friendly with me when we are alone. He kneads on me with the blanket and even purrs softly. Very nice, but not very Wolfie-ish.

3/27/99   Wolfie is much more comfortable with the others and vice versa. Last week (one week ago), Wolfie jumped up on the couch where Java was lying and started grooming Java. Actually, Wolfie laid right across Java first, then started grooming him. Wolfie went at this with vigor and I think this scared Java. Java did the bite thing on Wolfie's neck and then ran away up the tall carpeted kitty tree. Since this rattled them all, I got some more treats to take their minds off of things. It worked! No difficulties later. Right now, Java and India are off of their leashes and harnesses. I am comfortable with Java being loose and had no choice but to do the same with India since she took her second story flight to the bottom and bruised her lung. (She fell from the second floor and hit a piece of furniture. I took her in to Dr. Gordon's, where they examined and x-rayed her. No harness for this girl as she is too sore.) India doesn't seem too concerned with Wolfie but is also not 100 percent comfortable. Blanca is the least integrated, therefore the leash stays on her. I don't want her to leave the room. We are going very slowly, maybe a little too slowly, but it's better than starting all over again! Learned that lesson the hard way! We play with the fishing pole toy and its stick under a towel or carpet. They enjoy the stick—just like when they were little.

6/2/99   Spoke with Dr. Gordon today. The creatnine levels for all of the cats is too high, between 2.4 and 3.3. I need
to reduce their protein by 50 percent so this affects the treats
I give them. I have really reduced the turkey to a small amount.
I have also reduced the amount of turkey and salmon they eat
each day in their normal meals. (Remember, my cats are holistic cats. I make their food at every meal. No cat food here.
Everything is 100 percent edible by humans and is also as organic as I can get it.) When I hooked everyone up on their
leashes and harnesses tonight they got only 25 percent of the
normal amount of treats (deli turkey) and were okay with this.
After treats we played with the fishing pole and the metallic
spangle attachment. Wolfie is very comfortable, plays well even
on his leash. The only one who doesn't play is India. She typically does not hiss, but doesn't play either. India is basically a
lazy cat and is not as playful as Java and Blanca. India has come
face to face with Wolfie several times, usually it's okay. Blanca
hissed at Wolfie tonight but no big deal. We have finally made
very good progress. They are fairly comfortable together. I
think we need to move to the next step. Last weekend Wolfie
was hooked up and the others were free. This went well too.
Wolfie is a very nice cat and Java is a little love bug (loves to
rub up on me and always wants attention).

6/8/99   Exercises are going well on a daily basis. We use a
small amount of turkey for a treat and we play with the fishing
pole. Java, Wolfie, and Blanca all enjoy the spangle toy very
much. India couldn't care less. India is now the least integrated.
About two weeks ago Blanca became very outgoing. She often
comes to visit Wolfie in the bathroom in the morning. I have
been hooking up Java, Blanca, and India in the living room,
and while they are hooked up (secured) I let Wolfie explore
their bedroom. I want to get past the territory issue of bedroom and bathroom. Wolfie is interested in the bedroom,

smells a lot of things. Wolfie walked around the living room while the other three were secured. Seemed to work well. Blanca pulled out of her harness again, but she did not seem concerned with Wolfie being free. All are doing extremely well. Last weekend I let Wolfie out on his leash in the morning to give him a longer period of time with the others. We need to increase time spent together. Tonight, as I made dinner, Wolfie was hooked up while the others were free. The three chose to be in the kitchen while I was making their dinner. Again, all went well.

6/19/99   Well, all four cats are out. Wolfie is on his harness and a very long leash. Actually, I hooked three leashes up together to give him good length to walk around. I had them all out while I made their breakfast (it's Saturday, so no hurry). Wolfie was on the leash with me holding it while he walked around (walking on the leash like a dog). Wolfie decided to lie on top of the refrigerator. The other three were on the floor. All was fine. After feeding (Wolfie eats in the bathroom and the three were in the kitchen), Blanca went to the bathroom door and wanted in. I was not in the bathroom but she still wanted in. Over the last two days she has taken to coming into the bathroom in the morning with me and Wolfie. She will lie down on the counter with Wolfie but not right next to him. All is okay, unless he gets really close too many times. Very interesting, as she was initially my most resistant cat.

6/19/99 continued.   Java is doing well. He smells Wolfie the most. I don't think he has hissed in a while. Java is sleeping next to me on the couch while Wolfie is in his usual spot on the floor (next to the entertainment center with his back against it). Wolfie looks pretty relaxed. Ears are okay, he is cleaning himself. His tail is wiggling just a little. I think this is okay. In fact, he has stopped his tail now. All three cats are in his view.
  Blanca is doing well. She is comfy enough to sleep with Wolfie around. She only hisses if Wolfie persists in getting too

close too many times. She is the most sociable, as she comes into rooms that he is in. This morning we were in the bedroom and she came in and lay down there.

India is a bit of a mystery. She doesn't hiss at Wolfie, but she does not seek him out. She will get within a few feet of him, maybe two or three feet.

I am satisfied with the progress we have made. It is slow, but if I had gone more slowly to start with we would probably be done by now. All are doing okay on the reduced protein diet. I have increased the amount of veggies in their meals considerably; I give them about two ounces now. I have found that they all like to eat the fresh veggies alone. Kind of surprised me.

6/30/99   This last weekend (6/26 forward) I started letting all cats out together without being hooked up, but only while I am able to check on them. I am doing this only in the mornings and evenings when I am home. There has been minimal hissing, mainly from India. Wolfie is doing very well. He is very mellow. Yippee!

Around mid-July I gradually kept all cats out together for longer periods of time. One weekend toward the end of the month, I let them all stay out for the entire day. This way I could check in on them while I was running around doing errands. This is okay. I have kept both kitty pans even though they didn't have a problem originally with just one. They do use both pans and both are changed, not just cleaned, daily same as before. I have found that feeding them together is also an important thing. If Java and Wolfie can eat together peacefully, then all is well. If they can't then something is amiss.

Although Wolfie and the others are not as close as they were before the "incident," they are okay together now. Wolfie still prefers to lie atop the fridge. Java doesn't care. They are not buddies but they coexist together okay. Java has become much more possessive of me, but Wolfie doesn't seem to mind. Wolfie is not as friendly with me while the others are out. But, if it is just Wolfie and me, he will come up and talk to me and lie on me if I am on the couch. If I am in the bathroom, he chats up a storm. He rubs his head on me and even lies down while I am petting him so that I can rub his tummy and his back. It seems that the BuSpar somehow allowed him to create a better bond with me. You would never consider him a very loving, outgoing cat, but he is much better than before. Also, I don't want to mislead anyone, all of my cats are still big chickens. They don't do well around other people and are scared when they hear loud noises. They all get into their harnesses without any wiggling or any problems. They have come to accept harnesses with turkey. In fact, Wolfie gets excited when his harness is brought out.

11/20/99   Since the end of the summer to date, there have been a couple of incidents where I have had to separate Wolfie from the others. On both occasions, when I came home from work, everyone greeted me at the door except Wolfie. When I called him and he didn't come I would look for him. In both instances, I found him in the kitchen up on the cabinets. He considers this to be the safest place to hide, as he can back into a corner and see out. Also, no one gets up to the top of the cupboard easily.

Both times required giving Wolfie half of a 10 mg. tablet of Acepromozine to calm him down a little. Both times. After a little cooling-off time, I tried letting Wolfie out of the bathroom. Both times, it didn't go well. So, we took a few steps backward and gave everyone some time. After two days, I brought out the harnesses and leashes and hooked everyone up and gave them turkey treats. Remember, turkey treats are the greatest, as they (the cats) love them so much that they don't care about anything else. So, we spent about one week each time working on our exercises of having treats, playing, and just being out all together. While doing this, I would keep them separated during the day while I was at work. Every day

I would try feeding Wolfie with the others. If there was too much discomfort, hissing, or crying, then I would put Wolfie in the bathroom to eat. I have found when they can eat together peacefully, then they can be together the rest of the time.

So, I watch their body language and I make sure that all are relaxed. If one is not, then I pay particular attention to that cat. Usually, a little turkey and playing with the fishing pole toy makes them all forget whatever was bothering them. I have noticed that they have seen the cat the that initially caused the problem. They have seen this cat several times outside of the living room window. In fact, they even saw this cat on the porch (where they initially saw the intruder cat) and have gotten used to seeing her there. She is not there daily, but she does come to visit. This other cat seems to be interested in my four and she sits outside the window and cries. (Her owner is not home much.) They just look at her now.

I am not sure what upsets the boys (Java and Wolfie) when things do go wrong. If I am home and they get into a tiff I give them . . . you guessed it, a little treat, or I try to involve them in play. Each time we have had serious setbacks has been while I was at work.

Overall, I am very grateful for your initial visit and recommendations. I have learned more than you could possibly imagine. I know so much more about cats now. I have read every book I could lay my hands on. All in all, Wolfie is probably a better-adjusted cat. I can go out for the evening and then come home later and find all four cats on the bed. Last week, I found Wolfie, Java, and Blanca all lumped together in one ball. Again, although they don't have the same relationship as before, it is pretty good now. Wolfie occassionally plays with the others when they are batting around a wadded-up paper ball. He never did this before.

I realize that I can come home any day and expect setbacks; however, I love my cats and I understand them much better. I can look at their faces, ears, and tails and know if there is a problem, or if they are okay. I know that anyone going through this has to be willing to work with their cats and also have a good amount of patience. For me, there was no question. No one was going to be given away. I could not have made such a choice. I made a commitment when I decided to take them and I realize that it is a lifelong commitment . . . their lives, being long and healthy ones.

Between you and Dr. Gordon, we were able to get through this nightmare. I'm not joking, it was a nightmare to me. I have found a few people who understand how important it was to work this all out, and then, of course, there are people who think I am absolutely nuts. Too bad for them, I say. :^) Again, thanks so much.

—L. H.
11/20/99

NOTES

The following books and articles were used in researching this book. In some cases, a partial citation was given within the chapter itself. In other cases, the authors referred to a statistic, fact, or opinion without attribution within the chapter.

CHAPTER 1

Cat Ownership Demographics

"Man's Best Friend Gets the Girl," American Animal Hospital Association, *1995 Pet Owners Survey Human/Animal Bond,* 1995.

U.S. Pet Ownership and Demographics Sourcebook, American Veterinary Medical Association, Center for Information Management, Schaumburg, Ill., 1997.

Jungian Analytic Psychology, Archetypes, Personality Types, and Codependency

Animus and Anima, Emma Jung, Spring Publications Inc., Dallas, Texas, 1957.

Beneath the Mask: An Introduction to Theories of Personality, Christopher F. Monte, Harcourt Brace Jovanovich, Fort Worth, Texas, 1991.

Codependent No More: How to Stop Controlling Others and Start

Caring for Yourself, Melody Beattie, A Hazelden Book, HarperCollins, New York, 1987.

"Compliance Patterns," Codependents Anonymous handout, Phoenix, Ariz., 1988.

Dogs on the Couch: Behavior Therapy for Training and Caring for Your Dog, Larry Lachman and Frank Mickadeit, Overlook Press, New York, 1999.

Facing Codependence: What It Is, Where It Comes From, How It Sabotages Our Lives, Pia Mellody, Andrea Wells Miller, and J. Keith Miller, Harper, San Francisco, Cal., 1989.

Jung for Beginners, Jon Platania, Writers and Readers Publishing Inc., New York, 1997.

Please Understand Me, David Keirsey, Prometheus Nemesis Books, Del Mar, Cal., 1978.

Psychology, Lester M. Sdorow, WCB Brown & Benchmark Pubs., Dubuque, Iowa, 1993.

Theories of Personality, Calvin Springer Hall, Gardener Lindzey, John Campbell, John Wiley & Sons, 1978.

Family Systems Therapy

Families and Family Therapy, Salvador Minuchin, Harvard University Press, Cambridge, Mass., 1974.

CHAPTER 2

Cat Mythology

Cat Facts, Marcus Schneck and Jill Caravan, Barnes and Noble Books, New York, 1990 and 1993.

Cat World: A Feline Encyclopaedia, Desmond Morris, Penguin Books Ltd., Middlesex, England, 1996.

The Mythology of Cats: Feline Legend and Lore Through the Ages, Gerald and Loretta Hausman, St. Martin's Press, New York, 1998.

Understanding Your Cat, Michael Fox, Bantam, New York, 1974.

Prejudice and Stereotyping
The Nature of Prejudice, Gordon W. Allport, Doubleday, 1958.
Preventing Prejudice: A Guide for Counselors and Educators, Joseph G. Ponterotto and Paul B. Pedersen, Sage Publications, Newbury Park, Cal., 1993.

CHAPTER 3

Cats and Their Territory
CatSmart: The Ultimate Guide to Understanding, Caring for, and Living with Your Cat, Myrna Milani, Contemporary Books, 1998.
Cat Talk: What Your Cat Is Trying to Tell You, Carol C. Wilbourn, Publishers Choice, 1979.

CHAPTER 4

Cat and Their Territory
Cat Behavior: The Predatory and Social Behavior of Domestic and Wild Cats, Paul Leyhausen, Garland Press, New York, 1979.
Understanding Your Cat, Michael Fox, Bantam, New York, 1974.

Introducing a New Cat
Cat Talk: What Your Cat Is Trying to Tell You, Carol C. Wilbourn, Publishers Choice, 1979.

CHAPTER 5

American Cat Fanciers Association, P.O. Box 203, Point Lookout, Missouri, 65726. Phone: (417) 334–5430, FAX: (417) 334–5540, Email: *info@acfacat.com*

Cat Care Society, 5985 W. 11th Ave., Lakewood, Colo.,
    80214, (303) 239–9690.
The Cat Fanciers' Association Inc., P.O. Box 1005, Manas-
    quan, N.J. 08736–0805. Phone: (732) 528-9797, FAX: (732)
    528-7391, Web site: *www.cfainc.org*
Ralston-Purina Cat Training page, http://www.purina.com/
    cats/training/training.html

CHAPTER 6

Number of Cat Bites in U.S. Annually
Is Your Cat Crazy? John C. Wright, Castle Books, Edison, New
    Jersey, 1998.

Why Cats Bite
Cornell Feline Health Center, Cornell University College of
    Veterinary Medicine.
Cat Fanciers Association, Dr. Suzanne Hetts, P.O. Box 1005,
    Manasquan, N.J. 08736–0805. Phone: (732) 528-9797,
    FAX: (732) 528-7391, Web site: *www.cfainc.org*
Catlore, Desmond Morris, Jonathan Cape Ltd., London, 1987.
Cat World: A Feline Encyclopedia, Desmond Morris, Penguin
    Books Ltd., Middlesex, England, 1996.

Importance of Kitten Socialization
Understanding Your Cat, Michael Fox, Bantam, New York,
    1974.

CHAPTER 7

CatSmart, Myrna Milani, Contemporary Books, 1998.

Cat Declawing

Catlore, Desmond Morris, Johnathan Cape Ltd, London 1987.
Cat Talk, Carol C. Wilbourn, Publishers Choice, 1979.

CHAPTER 8

Meta-Communication

Understanding Your Cat, Michael Fox, Bantam, New York, 1974.

Cat Vocabulary

Catlore, Desmond Morris, Johnathan Cape Ltd., London, 1987.

CHAPTER 9

Stages of Child Development and Theories of Jean Piaget

Beneath the Mask: An Introduction to Theories of Personality, Christopher F. Monte, Harcourt Brace Jovanovich, Fort Worth, Texas, 1991.
Psychology, Lester M. Sdorow, WCB Brown & Benchmark Pubs., Dubuque, Iowa, 1993.

Child-Cat Interaction

Shelter Cats: Adopting from a Shelter, Selecting Your Cat, Cat Basics. Karen Commings, Howell Book House, New York, 1998.

Reasons People Give Up Their Pets

1995 Pet Owners Survey, Human Animal Bond, American Animal Hospital Association, 1995.

CHAPTER 10

Historical Cat-Phobic Figures
Cat World: A Feline Encyclopedia, Desmond Morris, Penguin
Books, Ltd., Middlesex, England, 1996.

Definitions of Anxiety Disorders, Behavior Therapy, and Cognitive-Behavior Therapy
Anxiety Disorders and Phobias: A Cognitive Perspective, Aaron T.
Beck M.D. and Gary Emery Ph.D., Basic Books, New York,
1985.
Diagnostic and Statistical Manual of Mental Disorders-DSM-IV,
American Psychiatric Ass'n, APA, Washington, D.C., 1994.
Feeling Good: The New Mood Therapy, David Burns M.D., Sig-
net Books, New York, 1980.
The Practice of Behavior Therapy, third ed., Joseph Wolpe, M.D.,
Pergamon Press, New York, 1982.

Age at Which Children Develop Certain Fears
"Fears and Phobias in Childhood," Michael Ferrari, *Child Psychiatry and Human Development,* Volume 17, 1986, p. 75.

Common Ways to Treat Phobias
"The Determinants and Treatment of Simple Phobias," S.
Rachman, *Advances in Behavior Research and Therapy,* Volume
13, 1990, pp. 1–30.

Use of Virtual Reality Therapy to Treat Cat Phobias
"Virtual reality therapy: An effective treatment for phobias,"
M. M. North, S. M. North, and J. R. Coble, *Student Health
Technology Information Journal,* 1998, Volume 58, pp. 112–
119.

Case of the Cat-Phobic Nurse
"Severe Cat Phobia," R. Blakey and K. Greig, *Nursing Times,*
July 1977, Volume 73, Number 29, pp. 1106–08.

CHAPTER 11

Diagnostic and Statistical Manual of Mental Disorders IV, American Psychiatric Ass'n, APA, Washington D.C., 1994.

Dogs on the Couch: Behavior Therapy for Training and Caring for Your Dog, Larry Lachman and Frank Mickadeit, Overlook Press, New York, 1999.

Dr. Pitcairn's Complete Guide to Natural Health for Dogs and Cats, Richard H. Pitcairn D.V.M. and Susan Hubble Pitcairn D.V.M., Rodale Press, Emmaus, Pa., 1995.

Handbook of Clinical Psychopharmacology for Therapists, John Preston Ph.D., John H. O'Neal M.D. and Mary C. Talaga B. S. Pharm., R.Ph., M.A., New Harbinger Publications, Oakland, Cal., 1994.

Synopsis of Psychiatry: Behavioral Sciences/Clinical Psychiatry, seventh ed., Harold I. Kaplan M.D., Benjamin J. Sadock M.D., and Jack A. Grebb M.D. Williams & Wilkins, Baltimore, Md., 1984.

CHAPTER 12

Phases of Grief

Death: The Final Stage of Growth. Elisabeth Kübler-Ross, Prentice-Hall, Inc., Englewood Cliffs, N.J., 1975.

Grief Counseling and Grief Therapy: A Handbook for the Mental Health Practioner, William J. Worden, Springer Publishing Co., New York, 1991.

How to Go on Living When Someone You Love Dies, Therese A. Rando, Bantam Books, New York, 1988, 1991.

Voices of Death, Edwin S. Shneidman, Harper & Row, New York, 1980.

Six Phases of Grief Larry Lachman Believes Are Most Accurate

After the Diagnosis: From Crisis to Personal Renewal for Patients with Chronic Illness, JoAnn LeMaistre, Ulysses Press, Berkeley, Cal., 1995.

Surviving Grief and Learning to Live Again, Catherine M. Sanders, John Wiley & Sons Inc., New York, 1992.

Other resources used in this chapter

Dogs on the Couch: Behavior Therapy for Training and Caring for Your Dog.

"Grief Is OK When You Lose a Pet," Bettijane Levine, *Los Angeles Times,* May 3, 1999, p. E-2.

"Saying Farewell to Fido," Edward Lewine, *The New York Times,* November 22, 1998.

CHAPTER 13

Parapsychology: A Century of Inquiry, D. Scott Rogo, Dell, New York, 1975.

Understanding Your Cat, Michael Fox, Bantam, New York, 1974.

The Signet Handbook of Parapsychology, Martin Ebon, Signet, New York, 1978.

Catlore, Desmond Morris, Jonathan Cape, Ltd., London, 1987.

"Dear Dr. Petshrink: Help! My Cat Is Driving Me Crazy," Joe Sharkey, *The New York Times,* January 10, 1999.

Flim-Flam: The Truth About Unicorns, Parapsychology and Other Delusions, James Randi, Lippincott & Crowell, New York, 1980.

Freud, Jung and Occultism, Nandor Fodor, University Books, New Hyde Park, NY, 1971.

"Influence of Companion Animals on the Physical and Psychological Health of Older People: An Analysis of a One-Year Longitudinal," P. Raina and colleagues, *Journal of the*

American Geriatric Society, March 1999.

Psychic Exploration, Martin Ebon and Edgar D. Mitchell, G. P. Putnam, New York, 1974.

The Roots of Coincidence: An Excursion into Parapsychology, Arthur Koestler, Vintage Books, New York, 1972.

BIBLIOGRAPHY AND
SUGGESTED READING

Allport, Gordon W. *The Nature of Prejudice*. New York: Doubleday, 1958.

American Animal Hospital Association. "Man's Best Friend Gets the Girl." *1995 Pet Owners Survey Human/Animal Bond.*

American Psychiatric Association. *Diagnostic and Statistical Manual of Mental Disorders IV*. Washington, D.C.: American Psychiatric Association, 1994.

American Veterinary Medical Association. *U.S. Pet Ownership and Demographics Sourcebook*. Schaumburg, Ill.: Center for Information Management, 1997.

Armstrong, Samantha. *Cat Quotations: A Collection of Lovable Cat Pictures and the Best Cat Quotes*. Watford, England: Exley Publications, 1992.

Aronson, Elliot, ed. *Readings About the Social Animal*. New York: W. H. Freeman, 1995.

Beattie, Melody. *Codependent No More: How to Stop Controlling Others and Start Caring for Yourself*. New York: Harper-Collins, 1987.

Beck, Aaron T., M. D., and Gary Emery, Ph.D. *Anxiety Disorders and Phobias: A Cognitive Perspective*. New York: Basic Books, 1985.

Becker, Marty, D.V.M. *Chicken Soup for the Cat and Dog Lover's Soul*. Deerfield Beach, Fla.: Health Communications, 1999.

Becker, Marty, D.V.M. *Chicken Soup for the Pet Lover's Soul.* Deerfield Beach, Fla.: Health Communications, 1998.

Berwick, Ray. *Ray Berwick's Complete Guide to Training Your Cat.* Tucson, Ariz.: H. P. Books, 1986.

Blakey, R., and K. Greig. "Severe Cat Phobia." *Nursing Times* 73 (July 1977): 1106-8.

Burns, David, M.D. *Feeling Good: The New Mood Therapy.* New York: Signet, 1980.

Capuzzo, Michael, and Teresa Banik-Capuzzo. *Cat Caught My Heart: Stories of Wisdom, Hope, and Purrfect Love.* New York: Bantam, 1998.

Commings, Karen. *Shelter Cats: Adopting from a Shelter, Selecting Your Cat, Cat Care Basics.* Foster City, Calif.: IDG Books Worldwide, 1998.

———. *The Shorthaired Cat: An Owner's Guide to a Happy Healthy Pet.* Foster City, Calif.: IDG Books Worldwide, 1996.

"Compliance Patterns". (CoDA handout). Phoenix, Ariz.: Codependents Anonymous, 1988.

Cosgrove, Melba. *How to Survive the Loss of a Love.* New York: Bantam, 1976.

Ebon, Martin, ed. *The Signet Handbook of Parapsychology.* New York: Signet, 1978.

Eisen, Armand. *Cat Chat: A Treasury of Feline Quotations.* Kansas City, Mo.: Ariel Books, 1997.

Ferrari, Michael. "Fears and Phobias in Childhood." *Child Psychiatry and Human Development* 17 (1986): 75.

Fox, Dr. Michael W. *Understanding Your Cat.* New York: Bantam, 1974.

Hall, Bill. "A Real Man Hides Behind a Cat." *The Lewiston Tribune.* Column 29A, from the *Bill Hall's Cat Tales Web Site* at: *http://netnow.micron.net/~philco/billhall/cats.htm*

Hall, Calvin S., and Gardner Lindzey. *Theories of Personality.* 3d ed. New York: John Wiley & Sons, 1978.

Hausman, Gerald, and Loretta Hausman. *The Mythology of Cats: Feline Legend and Lore Through the Ages.* New York: St. Martin's Press, 1998.

Jennings, L. B. "Potential Benefits of Pet Ownership in Health Promotion." *Journal of Holistic Nursing* 15, no. 4 (1997): 358–72.

Jung, Emma. *Animus and Anima*. Dallas: Spring Publications, 1957.

Kaplan, Harold I., et al. *Synopsis of Psychiatry: Behavioral Sciences/Clinical Psychiatry*. 7th ed. Baltimore: Kay, Williams & Wilkins, 1994.

Kay, William. *Pet Loss and Human Bereavement*. Ames: Iowa State University Press, 1995.

Keirsey, David. *Please Understand Me*. Del Mar, Calif.: Prometheus Nemesis Books, 1978.

Koestler, Arthur. *The Roots of Coincidence: An Excursion into Parapsychology*. New York: Vintage Books, 1972.

Kübler-Ross, Elisabeth. *On Death and Dying*. New York: Macmillan, 1969.

Lachman, Dr. Larry, and Frank Mickadeit. *Dogs on the Couch: Behavior Therapy for Training and Caring for Your Dog*. New York: Overlook Press, 1999.

Landrine, Hope, ed. *Bringing Cultural Diversity to Feminist Psychology: Theory, Research, and Practice*. Washington, D.C.: American Psychological Association, 1995.

Layton, C. T. "Pasteurella Multocida Meningitis and Septic Arthritis Secondary to a Cat Bite." *Journal of Emergency Medicine* 17, no. 3 (1999): 445–8.

LeMaistre, JoAnn. *After the Diagnosis: From Crisis to Personal Renewal for Patients with Chronic Illness*. Berkeley, Calif.: Ulysses Press, 1995.

Levine, Bettijane. "Grief Is OK When You Lose a Pet." *Los Angeles Times*, 3 May 1999, sec. E, p. 2.

Lewine, Edward. "Saying Farewell to Fido." *New York Times*, 22 November 1988.

Leyhausen, Paul. *Cat Behavior: The Predatory and Social Behavior of Domestic and Wild Cats*. New York: Garland Press, 1979.

Lipsyte, Robert. "Coping: Bonding With an Aloof King of the Urban Jungle." *New York Times*, 6 June 1999.

Mellody, Pia, et al. *Facing Codependence: What It Is, Where It Comes from, How It Sabotages Our Lives*. San Francisco: Harper San Francisco, 1998.

Milani, Myrna, D.V.M. *CatSmart: The Ultimate Guide to Understanding, Caring for, and Living with Your Cat*. Chicago: Contemporary Books, 1998.

Minuchin, Salvador. *Families and Family Therapy*. Cambridge, Mass.: Harvard University Press, 1974.

Mitchell, Edgar D., and John White. *Psychic Exploration: A Challenge for Science*. New York: G. P. Putnam's Sons, 1974.

Monte, Christopher F. *Beneath the Mask: An Introduction to Theories of Personality*. Fort Worth: Harcourt Brace Jovanovich, 1991.

Morris, Desmond. *Catlore*. London, England: Jonathan Cape, 1987.

———. *Cat World: A Feline Encyclopedia*. Harmondsworth, England: Penguin Books, 1996.

Nash, Bruce, and Allan Zullo. *Amazing but True Cat Tales*. Kansas City, Mo.: Andrews & McMeel, 1993.

North, M. M., et al. "Virtual Reality Therapy: An Effective Treatment for Phobias." *Student Health Technology Information Journal* 58 (1998): 112–19.

Patronek, G. J., et al. "Risk Factors for Relinquishment of Cats to an Animal Shelter." *Journal of the American Veterinary Medical Association* 209, no. 3 (1996): 582–88.

Pitcairn, Richard H., D.V.M., and Susan Hubble Pitcairn, D.V.M. *Dr. Pitcairn's Complete Guide to Natural Health for Dogs and Cats*. Emmaus, Pa.: Rodale Press, 1995.

Platania, Jon, Ph.D. *Jung for Beginners*. New York: Writers and Readers Publishing, 1997.

Ponterotto, Joseph G., and Paul B. Pedersen. *Preventing Prejudice: A Guide for Counselors and Educators*. Newbury Park, Calif.: Sage Publications, 1993.

Quackenbush, Jamie. *When Your Pet Dies: How to Cope with Your Feelings*. New York: Simon & Schuster, 1985.

Rachman, S. "The Determinants and Treatment of Simple Phobias." *Advances in Behavior Research and Therapy* 13 (1990): 1–30.

Randi, James. *Flim-Flam: The Truth About Unicorns, Parapsychology, and Other Delusions.* New York: Lippincott & Crowell, 1980.

Rando, Therese A. *How to Go On Living When Someone You Love Dies.* New York: Bantam, 1991.

Robbins, Maria Polushkin. *Puss in Books: A Collection of Great Cat Quotations.* Hopewell, N.J.: Ecco Press, 1994.

Editors of Pets Part of the Family Books. *Pets Part of the Family: The Total Care Guide for All the Pets in Your Life.* Emmaus, Pa.: Rodale Press, 1999.

Rogo, D. Scott. *Parapsychology: A Century of Inquiry.* New York: Dell, 1975.

Rubin, Sheldon. *Practical Guide to Cat Care.* Lincolnwood, Ill.: Publications International, 1995.

Sanders, Catherine M. *Surviving Grief and Learning to Live Again.* New York: John Wiley & Sons, 1992.

Schneck, Marcus, and Jill Caravan. *Cat Facts.* New York: Barnes & Noble Books, 1993.

Shneidman, Edwin S. *Voices of Death.* New York: Harper & Row, 1980.

Sdorow, Lester M. *Psychology.* 4th ed. Burr Ridge, Ill.: WCB/McGraw-Hill, 1999.

Torregrossa, Richard. *Fun Facts About Cats: Inspiring Tales, Amazing Feats, and Helpful Hints.* Deerfield Beach, Fla.: Health Communications, 1998.

Ward, Amy. *The Healthy Dog and Cat Book.* New York: Pinnacle Books, 1983.

White-Bowden, Susan. *The Barn Cat, Sassy, and a Guardian Angel: Heroic Animal Tales.* Baltimore: Gateway Press, 1998.

Whiteley, H. Ellen. *Understanding and Training Your Cat or Kitten.* New York: Crown, 1994.

Wilbourn, Carole C. *Cat Talk: What Your Cat Is Trying to Tell You.* New York: Publishers Choice, 1991.

Wilbourn, Carole C. *Cats on the Couch: The Complete Guide for Loving and Caring for Your Cat.* New York: Humane Society of New York, 1982.

Wolpe, Joseph, *The Practice of Behavior Therapy.* 3d ed. New York: Pergamon Press, 1982.

Worden, J. William. *Grief Counseling and Grief Therapy: A Handbook for the Mental Health Practitioner.* New York: Springer, 1991.

Wright, John C., Ph.D. *Is Your Cat Crazy?* Edison, N.J.: Castle Books, 1998.

INDEX

impacted anal glands and soiling
problems, 49
Inderal, 76–77
Index of Famous Cats, 150
Innocent VIII, Pope, 15
insecticides and safety, 29
interdependence (and pet ownership)
characteristics of, 6
vs. co-dependence, 4–6
the domestic cat and, 7–8
intermittent depression and the grief
process, 130
International Cat Association, The
(TICA), 147
Cat Fanciers Web Site, 150
International Veterinary Acupuncture
Society (IVAS)), 147
intuition
as a human personality trait, 8–9
Iproniazid, 114
isolation and the grief process, 129

jealousy
cats and phone conversations, 8
Jones, Ernest, 136–37
Jung, Carl, 2, 8, 9
Jung, Emma, 155
Jungian analytic psychology, concepts
of, 154

Karen Commings Cat Auther Web
Site, 150
Katascali Birman Cattery, 150
Keirsey, David, 9
Keirsey Temperament Sorter, 9
Kubaryk, Aaron, 101
Kübler-Ross, Elisabeth, 126

Larry's Family Animal Web Site, 150
lazy, myth of cat's as, 17
Leyhausen, Paul, 1
Librium, 114
litter box problems
behavior therapy for, 50–56
medication and remedies, 56
psychical causes, 48–49

psychological and behavioral, 49–
50
soiling (case files), 22–23, 29, 45–
46, 46–47, 59
See also spraying and marking
lorazepam (Ativan), 119
Louis XIV, 16

McDougall, William, 135
McMillan, Stuart, 81
Magic of Uri Geller, The (Randi), 138,
139
marking and spraying, 56–57
case files, 47, 59
neutering and spaying, 58
See also litter box problems
Mather, Increase, 103
Mayer-Briggs Type Indicator, 9
meanness. See aggression.
medications
allergic reactions, 116
discontinuance reactions, 116
effects of, 115–16
and safety, 28
See also mental health
mental health, 113–33
anti-anxiety drugs, 119
antidepressants, 114, 118–19
case files, 113–14, 122
chemical messengers in the brain,
117–18
drugs, deciding on, 121
drugs as treatment, 114, 120
holistic approach, 120–21
other considerations, 121–22
meowing and crying (chronic),
81–89
behavior modification for, 85–87
calls, meaning of, 82–84
case files, 81–82, 89
medication and, 87
premature weaning and, 85–86
punishment as a last resort, 8–88
stress-induced, 81–82, 89
meta-communication, 83
Mikes, George, 69